BEWARE! SATAN

Strategies of Defense

BEWARE! SATAN

Strategies of Defense

Mehmet Yavuz Şeker

Tughra Books

New Jersey

Published by Tughra Books

26 Worlds Fair Dr. Unit C

Somerset, New Jersey, 08873, USA

www.tughrabooks.com

Library of Congress Cataloging-in-Publication Data

Seker, Mehmet.
 Beware! Satan : strategies of defense / Mehmet Yavuz Seker.
    p. cm.
 Includes bibliographical references and index.
 ISBN 978-1-59784-131-3 (pbk.)
 1. Devil--Islam. 2. Devil--Islam--Koranic teaching. I. Title.
 BP166.89.S45 2008
 297.2'16--dc22

                                                    2008013783

Printed by
Çağlayan A.Ş., Izmir - Turkey
Sarnıç Yolu Üzeri No:7
Tel: (+90 232) 252 22 85
June 2008

CONTENTS

INTRODUCTION

Human beings have been created with distinction, blessed with physical and spiritual qualities and raised to the level of the noblest beings among all creation. Being the noblest also brings responsibilities; they are given a route to follow in which obedience is essential. Humans can only find true happiness in submission to God by being on His holy path. Deviation from the path results in such disorder and dismay that true happiness and peace cannot be reached.

Satan is the greatest obstacle on the path to success. He is a being in constant rebellion and thrives on egoism; so, he will use any means possible to drag humankind into his deviant path. The reason for this is that he cannot stand watching people succeed where he himself has failed, or be a bystander as people walk toward happiness in both this world and the other world by believing and obeying the commandments of their Lord.

Satan failed to understand the delicate situation of obedience and, as a result of the difficult test to which he was subjected, he turned away from the path and rebelled against the Almighty. However, this was not the end of it; he continued to defend his actions by producing excuses, which consequently determined his fate. He was cursed, expelled from Paradise and lost all he had. Although Adam was a mere tool in his test, Satan did not realize this and blamed Adam for his own faults and swore revenge against Adam and his progeny. This was the point where Satan closed all gates leading to good and, by using all his faculties for the purpose of evil, began an assault on humankind.

The great scholars of old gave the title *masawi al-akhlaq* to Satan, which meant "the source of all evil-manners."[1]

Having such a nemesis, human beings should be prepared for Satan's devious campaign by planning a strategy of defense and making lifelong plans in accordance with the purpose of their creation. If the strategy works and the instigation of Satan can be avoided, the mission is accomplished. However, if we fail and fall into Satan's trap, we will feel regret and a sense of despair in our hearts. This will eventually cause an inner deformation due to recurring contradictions with our nature. This internal unease may cause us to turn to our Lord in repentance and once again regain our composure. This repentance causes Satan's all efforts to misguide man away from his Lord to be wasted. Let us not forget that in order to attain the pleasure of God one must reject both the invitation of one's *nafs* (carnal self or worldly desires) and of Satan.

In the first chapter of this book, we examine the identity of Satan, the purpose and time of his creation and his interaction with Adam. In the second chapter, we scrutinize Satan's essence by examining the Holy Qur'an and the hadith. In chapter 3, we examine Satan's attributes and expose his methods. In chapter 4, we identify how Satan attempts to exploit our worship of God. Finally, in the last chapter, we seek ways in which to shield ourselves from the whispers of Satan by studying the ways of equipping ourselves with spiritual protection. Also, we emphasize the importance of taking refuge in God from the evil instigation of Satan.

In this work only authenticated hadith have been used as a resource. We have chosen to avoid going into the detailed analysis of the hadith recounted in this work in order to emphasize the importance of the issue.

Satan is clearly a tool of trial, appointed by God as an enemy which beleaguers man. Life in one aspect is a struggle between man and Satan. In order to succeed in life, knowing your enemy and developing strategies is one of the most important means. If this unpretentious book about Satan, who has dedicated his existence to destruction, supplies some useful information, then we will consider our efforts not to have been wasted. Effort and hard work are the duty of humans, whereas the results and the blessings of success belong to God.

Mehmet Yavuz Şeker

1

The Creation and Essence of Satan

Definition of the words Shaitan and Iblis

Shaitan

The word *shaitan* (in English, 'satan') is derived from an Arabic root and can be analyzed in various ways when the triconsonantal root is divided into its component parts. Focusing on the letter *n* in the final position, some linguists are inclined to derive the word from the verbal root *sh-t-n*, meaning, 'one who has gone astray or is distant.' Accordingly, *shaitan* (Satan) is one who has actually distanced himself from the Lord and His mercy. The term *shayatin* (plural for *shaitan*) supports this argument, as the plural form of the word also carries a very significant aspect of the meaning.

According to another view, the letter *n* in the final position is a non-root consonant and the actual root consisted of *sh-w-t*. In this case, the word *shaitan* means 'one burnt or doomed to perish.' Those who take the latter as the root base their claim on the fact that Satan was created from pure fire. They also support their argument by pointing out that Satan frequently utilizes the feelings of rage and wrath. As for controlling anger, the Prophet said, "Anger comes from Satan and Satan was created of fire."[1] On another occasion, the Prophet advised one of the Companions, whose face had become red with anger, to cool himself down by saying, "I seek refuge in God from Satan, the outcast."[2]

Abu Ubayda states, "The word 'satan' is a general term used to refer to all humans or animals who display evil, cunning, deceiving and misleading behavior." Zajjaj states that all things ugly and unpleasant resemble Satan: "When we come across an ugly thing, we liken it to the face of Satan. Satan is unseen but if we could see him, we would behold a horrible creature."[3]

The word 'satan' is used as a general term for extreme acts of evil, and it represents a creature of extreme wickedness and stubbornness. Its meaning includes all beings that possess a spiritual connection to evil; hence, humans, animals and unseen entities are included in this category.[4] Asim Efendi states in his *Qamus* that Satan was known as 'Azazil' before the expulsion from the Garden.[5]

Iblis

Although the name 'Iblis' is used often in place of 'Satan' and regarded as the same thing, from a linguistic point of view it does not carry the same meaning. There are also different views regarding the source of the word *Iblis*. Some claim that it is derived from the Arabic verbal root *b-l-s*, so the word *iblas* means 'one who has lost all hope of blessing' or 'one who is in despair.' They support their claim by arguing that after his rebellion, Iblis lost all hope in God's mercy, and hence this interpretation makes sense.

However, according to some, the word does not come from the Arabic language. Even though people claim that the name 'Iblis' comes from the root word *iblas*, many believe it was introduced from another language. Ismail ibn Hammad al-Jawhari, the renowned scholar of Arabic language also supports this view.[6] The name 'Iblis' is mentioned in eleven places in the Qur'an. Whenever the Qur'an mentions Satan's rebellion against God, it uses the name 'Iblis.'

THE ESSENCE OF SATAN

His own essence and nature

When we study the verses regarding the creation of Satan, we see that he was created from fire. In his own statement, Satan claims, "You have created me from fire."[7] When it comes to classifying him as a species, he belongs to the jinn, which were also created from fire:

> And (recall) when We said to the angels, "Prostrate before Adam!" and they all prostrated, but Iblis did not; he was of the jinn (created before humankind, from smokeless, scorching fire) and transgressed against his Lord's command. Will you, then, take him and his progeny for guardians (to rely on and refer your affairs to) rather than Me, when they are an enemy to you? How evil an exchange for the wrongdoers! (Kahf 18:50)

As shown clearly at the beginning of this verse, Iblis, who is one of the jinn, was ordered to bow down along with all the angels before Adam, but he left the straight path by refusing to obey. The latter part of the verse explains the wretchedness of turning away from God and joining Satan and his followers. Ibn Arabi states, "Iblis is a spirit which reflects God's name 'Mudhill' (the All-Abasing) in its best form."[8]

The Qur'an also gives a fuller account of the refusal of Iblis to prostrate before Adam at the time of the latter's creation:

> We brought you into existence, then We gave you each a form (perfectly suited to your nature), and then We said to the angels (to signify that they affirm the degree of knowledge and superiority of Adam and his deserving vicegerency, and that they will help him to perform his duty on the earth), "Prostrate before Adam!" They all prostrated, but Iblis did not; he was not of those who prostrated. He (God) said, "What prevented you from prostrating when I commanded you to do so?" Iblis said, "I am better than he, for You have created me from fire, and him You have created from clay." (God) said, "Then go down from it; it is not for you to act haughtily there! So be gone! Surely you are of the degraded." (Iblis) said, "Grant me respite till the Day when they will all be raised from the dead!" (God) said, "You shall be among the ones granted respite (so long as humankind remains on the earth)." (Iblis) continued, "Now that You have allowed me to rebel and go astray, I will surely lie in wait for them on Your Straight Path (to lure them from it). Then I will come upon them from before them and from behind

them, and from their right and from their left. And You will not find most of them thankful." (A'raf 7:11–17)[9]

We can conclude from these verses that the Almighty had not issued a command to Satan before the unfolding of this incident. Satan had not been subjected to a test prior to this incident. Perhaps he had carried out previous orders only because they did not involve the testing of his ego or arrogance, so they did not try his loyalty. Previously he had enjoyed a life among the angels where things were occurring in accordance to his wishes. He was in a situation where his loyalty was not questioned. The test of his loyalty came when Adam was created and they were all instructed to bow before him. This command brought out Satan's true nature and feelings. It unearthed his feelings of arrogance, so he refused to bow before Adam. Satan listened to his own ego and, in an attempt to justify his actions, he pointed to Adam and claimed, *"I am better than he!"* Thus, he both lied and demonstrated his ignorance.

The right thing to do was to submit to the will of God by displaying total obedience. Instead, Satan stood in rebellion and argued, using demagogy and comparison with deficient logic. He questioned Adam's value by emphasizing the creation of Adam. He argued that Adam was created of clay, whereas he was made of fire. His evaluation was based on materialism. He could not fathom the magnificence of God's creating a being out of clay and blowing a soul into it, or he simply did not wish to understand it. So, in an egoistic and arrogant manner, he claimed, *"I am better than he!"*

There is a lesson to be derived from Satan's request, *"Grant me respite till the Day when they will all be raised from the dead!"* Satan did not deny God, nor did he reject the Day of Judgment. He knew that Adam would have descendants and they would live for a certain period of time and then die to be resurrected once again. In fact, Adam had also made a mistake. However, unlike Satan, as soon as he realized his fault, he rushed to repent with his wife by his side as they straightaway said in remorse, *"Our Lord! We have wronged ourselves, and if You do not forgive us and do not have mercy on us, we will surely be among those who have lost!"* (A'raf 7:23).

At first, Satan's situation was no different from that of Adam and his wife; when Satan disobeyed, like Adam, he was not condemned immediately. He was interrogated and given a chance to explain himself. With atonement and remorse, he could have saved his soul. The signs were there, and he was even granted time. Yet, he stubbornly insisted on defying God. Consequently, he placed himself in a position where he was told, *"Then get you down out of it; surely you are one rejected (from My mercy)"* (Hijr 15:34; Sa'd 38:77). Therefore, he entered the path of eternal despair.[10] Having despaired of the mercy of God, there was nothing of good left in him; all faculties of good were blown out like the flame of a candle.

Contemporary scholar Fethullah Gülen analyzes this emotional stage of Satan with an analogy:

> Humans are revered beings and if they use the dynamics which they are gifted with in an appropriate manner, they can transform themselves into angelic beings. Now, think about a pious man who performs daily prayers in humility, observes the fast, goes on the holy pilgrimage and approaches everyone with compassion. Let us say that this unique individual was indiscriminately harassed, his integrity was questioned, his honor was destroyed, and he was not even valued as a human being. He was brought to a stage where his nervous system was loaded with mountainous rage and anger. Let us say he was like a ticking time bomb. In the heat of that moment of explosion, there would be no sign of tranquility, peace, mercy, or compassion in his mind. At that instant, if you analyzed this man's emotional state, you would see only rage and fury in the form of sparks such as the ones emitted by the flames of hell. No matter what kind of advice you put forward to him at that instant, it would have no effect. Every human being at some stage of their lives may experience such rage. Satan experiences such rage, anger, vengeance, and hatred every millisecond of his life. His body is totally infested by these types of emotions. Throughout his life, he thinks of nothing but evil. He is in such fury and paroxysm that he can bear no thoughts other than satanic ones. Since he is

full of evil, there is no room for good, so the opportunity to think about good never arises. This is why he denies God, although he knows Him. He is like the believer described above, but with constant vengeance and rage. He does not remember God, and hence he denies His existence because something inside prevents him from doing so.[11]

The degradation of Satan consists of two parts. The first part was his disobeying an order because of extreme conceit and relying on his own reasoning; his pride prevented him from prostrating before Adam. This was a situation where he should have obeyed unconditionally. In the second part, he was questioned about his disobedience and he chose to enter into dispute by proposing a comparison. He was granted a second chance, so all he had to do was to apologize and repent. The noble Prophet stated, "Satan is the first being who made a comparison."[12] Using his own flawed, misleading logic, Satan compared fire to clay and assumed that fire was far superior to clay. He argued, "*Shall I prostrate myself before one whom You created of clay?*" and "*Do You see this that You have honored above me?*" (Isra 17:61–62) With his disrespectful words, Satan dared to blame God for His decision by claiming that he was nobler than Adam.

This first comparison was made during a debate to defend his actions. Satan's mind was clouded with pride and this caused him to fall into a bottomless abyss. In a hadith reported by Anas ibn Malik, the noble Prophet states, "Iblis will wear the first garment made of fire."[13] So, on the Day of Judgment, the father of debaters shall be punished by wearing the first garment made out of his own essence—fire!

The essence and nature of his aids

As a result of failing his test, Satan was turned inside out, and all that he kept inside was now out on the surface. The contradictions embedded in his essence surfaced. There was no sign of remorse throughout all these events. He chose to exploit all his abilities in the name of evil. Consequently, he closed all gates opening to good and caused the decay of the seeds of good which had been originally placed in his essence. The end product was a being composed of nothing but evil.

This is Satan, who chooses his aids from among jinn and humans. He selects those who have closed their souls to repentance and those who have stained their conscience. He whispers fancy words into their hearts, asking them to join him. He then uses them for his devious plans. Joining forces with Satan, these individuals even harass Prophets:

> Likewise did We make for every Prophet a hostile opposition from among the satans of humankind and the jinn, whispering and suggesting to one another specious words by way of delusion. Yet had your Lord willed (and compelled everybody to behave in the way He wills), they would not have done it: so leave them alone with what they have been fabricating. And the hearts of those who do not believe in the Hereafter incline toward it (their deluding speech) and take pleasure in it, and they continue perpetrating the evils that they have long been perpetrating. (An'am 6:112–113)

As shown at the beginning of the verse above, whether human or jinn, those who display such behavioral traits as stubbornness, arrogance, instigation, treachery, hypocrisy and rebellion are considered to be satanic beings.[14] Ata, Mujahid and Qatada heard Ibn Abbas state, "There are jinn and human satans; if the jinn satan fails to deceive a believer, he will use a human satan to pester him." The noble Prophet asked Abu Dharr, "Have you taken refuge in God from the jinn and human satans?" Abu Dharr replied, "Is there a human satan?" The noble Prophet answered, "Yes, and they are more detrimental than the jinn."[15]

Creating a Satan for every Prophet from among the jinn and humankind is a law implemented by God in social life. The pharaoh, for instance, was the satan of Moses and Abu Jahl was the satan of Muhammad, upon whom be peace and blessings. In every period of history, good has been relentlessly challenged by evil.

This is a law placed in the universe by its Creator.[16] In the Qur'an, those who behave like Satan are described as satans:

> When they meet those who believe, they declare (hypocritically), "We believe," but when they are alone in secret with their (apparently human) satans, they say, "Assuredly we are with you; we (were) only jesting." (Baqara 2:14)

Those who give advice to hypocrites are also human beings, but they are described as '(human) satans' and this suggests that these evil ones are no different from Satan.

When they gather in their secret organizations and tutor their pupils of evil instigation, they say, "We are really with you; you can be sure of that." The use of *shayatin* ('satans' in the plural) in the verse above clearly shows that they are multiple in number.[17]

THE CREATION OF SATAN

The time of his creation

Let us briefly study the creation of humans before we scrutinize the time Satan was created. The creation of Adam occurred within a stretch of time. First, God gave potential to clay to be a human. Then, He created living cells from clay and these cells were subjected to many different processes and filtrations before a human form appeared: "*He created him from earth, then said to him, 'Be!' And he was*" (Imran 3:59). As the verse clearly suggests, Adam was created from the earth. This means that all human beings originated from the earth. In this process the soil was mixed with water first, and it became clay: "*I am creating a mortal (man) out of clay*" (Sad 38:71). Then, this mixture of water and soil dried, decomposed and developed the right components for living cells, which were then filtered: "*We created humankind (in the very beginning) from a specially sifted extract of clay*" (Mu'minun 23:12). Later, these refined cells would become a human being. This single man's partner was also produced from him: "*O humankind! In due reverence for your Lord, keep from disobedience to Him Who created you from a single human self, and from it created its mate*" (Nisa 4:1). Later joining with his mate he could begin to reproduce, "*and from the pair of them scattered abroad a multitude of men and women*" (Nisa 4:1).

So, humankind's origin lies within soil. The soil was transformed into clay and passed through a chemical process of purification where cells were filtered and perfected. Reproduction was based on the joining of male and female. A human being goes through particular stages in the mother's womb before becoming a human being. Just like their great ancestor Adam, human beings go through stages of creation. The holy Qur'an explains the stages of the development of the human embryo:

> O humankind! If you are in doubt about the Resurrection, (consider that) We created you from earth (in the beginning while there was nothing of your existence as humankind), and the material origin of every one of you is earth. Then (We have created you) from a drop of (seminal) fluid, then from a clot clinging (to the womb wall), then from a lump in part shaped and in part not shaped, and differentiated and undifferentiated, and so do We clarify for you. (Hajj 22:5)

Upon arrival in this world, a human being continues to travel through different stages. Following birth, we experience stages such as babyhood, childhood, adolescence, maturity and old age. Of course, that is if we do not meet death during one of the earlier stages. One should acknowledge God's power and divine wisdom by contemplating the fact that He converted soil into dried and decomposed clay, and from that He created man.[18]

The jinn, on the other hand, were created before humans, from an intense blaze of fire (*nar al-samum*). This is a unique fire with a venomous quality which would fry a human being instantly upon the slightest touch. Enes ibn Malik transmits a hadith which supports the earlier creation of Satan: "The Messenger of God said, 'When God created Adam and kept him in the Garden for a period of time, Satan constantly stalked him to discover his weaknesses. When he observed the emptiness in him, he realized that man was created weak, in such a way that he is incapable of controlling his carnal desires.'"[19]

Satan persistently stalked Adam, the father of humanity, trying to discover all the weak points of his future adversary. Satan's possession of such tactical knowledge suggests that he existed before Adam. As a matter of fact, all the verses which explain how Satan refused to bow down before Adam prove that he was created before humans.

The reasons for Satan's creation

When we observe our environment, we realize that everything is created with a divine purpose. No entity can be described as purposeless.[20] Therefore, there is also divine purpose in the creation of Satan.

First, as explained above, Satan was ordered to bow down before Adam, but his pride and arrogance overcame him and he became a stubborn, rebellious unbeliever. Since Adam was the tool which unearthed his feelings of rebellion and unbelief, he became his archenemy. Satan made an oath to lead humankind astray from the right path. Now, humankind became his eternal enemy, so he strives with all his capabilities to see his adversary suffer, both in this world and in the one after.[21] Being in this situation, facing such an enemy, humans should always be alert and forewarned. While we live in accordance with the purpose of our creation, we should utilize the control mechanism with which we have been blessed in the most efficient way possible.[22] This means the existence of Satan causes humans to lead lives of awareness and alertness.

Second, this world is a place of trial and testing: God *"has created death and life, so that He may try you (and demonstrate to yourselves) which of you is best in deeds"* (Mulk 67:2). So, we are faced with various tests that appear as means of assessment throughout our lives, and Satan is one of them.

Third, our Lord informs us of Satan's animosity toward man and instructs us also to declare him our enemy. What is expected of us is to oppose Satan and his beliefs and actions. We are expected to behave submissively to God, not to Satan. Evidently, this enhances our spiritual essence, bringing us closer to our Lord. Humans will only attain the highest level of humanity by contesting their eternal enemy. Bediüzzaman Said Nursi tackles the issue from a unique perspective:

> It is not an evil that God created and creates devils and apparently evil and disastrous acts, for they produce good and important results. For example, angels do not rise to the higher spiritual ranks because devils cannot tempt them into deviation. Animals have fixed stations, and so cannot rise to higher stations or fall to lower ones. But human beings can acquire endless ranks or stations, all the way from the top to the bottom. There is an infinitely long line of spiritual evolution between the ranks of the greatest Prophets and saints and such people as Pharaoh and Nimrod.
>
> Thus, this world is the field, and this life the term, in which people are tested so that elevated diamond-like spirits may be distinguished from base coal-like ones. This is why devils were created and Prophets were sent with Divine commandments. Without such testing, good and evil could not be distinguished and would be treated equally: the spirit of Abu Bakr, who rose to the highest level after the Prophets, would remain at the same level as that of Abu Jahl, who fell to the lowest level.[23] Thus, the creation of devils and evil is wholly good, for they cause good and universal results to be achieved. Those who suffer because of them do so because of their own weakness, misuse of their free will, or some external circumstances that they caused to appear. As a result, all evil and misfortune that happen to people lie in themselves, not in God's creation of them.
>
> If you ask: As sending Prophets has caused many or even most people to become unbelievers because of Satan's seduction, how can you say that creating evil things and acts is good, that raising Prophets is a mercy for humanity?
>
> Answer: As quality is always far more important than quantity, we should consider only qualitative values in making our judgment. To cite an example: 100 date stones are worth only

100 cents until they are planted and grow into palm trees. But if only 20 grow into trees and the remaining 80 rot because of over-watering, how can you say it is an evil to plant and water them? Everyone would agree that it is wholly good to have 20 trees at the expense of 80 date stones, since 20 trees will give 20,000 date stones. Again, 100 peacock eggs are worth maybe 500 cents. But if she sits on the eggs and only 20 hatch, who can say it is an evil that 80 eggs were spoiled in return for 20 peacocks? On the contrary, it is wholly good to have 20 peacocks at the expense of 80 eggs, because the 20 peacocks will be worth far more than the eggs and will lay more eggs.

And so it is with humanity. Our being raised up by Prophets, as well as our fight against Satan and our carnal self, result in the loss of animal-like people, unbelievers, and hypocrites (more in number but poorer in quality) in exchange for hundreds of thousands of Prophets, millions of saints, and billions of people of wisdom and sincerity—the suns, moons, and stars of the human world.[24]

Evidently, the creation of Satan and his aids is not evil, but following their path and becoming their dupes is evil.

Satan's interaction with Adam

When Adam was created, Satan was residing in heaven among the angels. As the angels were ordered to bow down before Adam, Satan was also among the addressees. However, his nature was different from that of the angels. The angels *"do not disobey God in whatever He commands them, and carry out what they are commanded (to carry out)"* (Tahrim 66:6). So, the angels, who received divine praise, immediately bowed down in prostration. Satan was the only being who refused and so prepared his own fate.

Prostration carries the meanings of respect, humility and submission. It is the opposite of arrogance. Literally, it can be interpreted as bowing down and placing the forehead on the ground. Since prostration has the meaning of surrendering and humility, it also means total submission of the heart to the One it is performed for. Although it is generally against Islam to prostrate before anyone but God, the prostration of the angels before Adam was a unique situation. The act should be evaluated from their own reality of agreeableness.[25] Disobedience by the angels was out of the question, since they receive pleasure out of inexorably serving God. If prostration is performed for God, it becomes worship.[26] When it is done for someone else, it carries the meaning of glorifying and honoring the one before whom it is performed. Prostration can also be a form of respect and admiration; this is the kind which was performed by his father and brothers to Prophet Joseph.[27]

The prostration of the angels before Adam was an act of honoring Adam, acknowledging his virtue and grace, and, more importantly, it was an act of worshipping God. Just as we turn toward the Ka'ba to worship God, after receiving their orders the angels regarded Adam as their *qibla* (the direction faced in the prayer). Hence they actually worshipped God in full submission to the order while bowing down before Adam.[28] Satan, however, did not bow to Adam and thus he disobeyed God. He did not comprehend the fine detail of obedience; therefore, he refused, rebelled and became an unbeliever. He did not become an unbeliever because he denied the existence of God, but because of his rebellion against Him. He refused to bow, even though acknowledging the divine truth.

Faith is a complete entity which cannot be divided. The rules and verdicts of Islam are also complete, and they cannot be divided. Denying a single ruling of religion means denying Islam altogether. If a person who believes in God and in the Day of Judgment refuses to accept a single verse from the Qur'an, he has stepped out of the holy circle of Islam. The same rule applies to someone who claims that something is lawful when God has clearly forbidden it. Satan had heard the commandment of God but disobeyed it. He belittled Adam, and thus he became the victim of his own egotism and haughtiness.

When Satan refused to prostrate before Adam, God Almighty said, *"O Adam, surely this is an enemy to you and your wife; so let him not drive the two of you out of the Garden, lest you become distressed"*

(Ta Ha 20:117). They were further warned, *"O Adam! Dwell you and your spouse in the Garden, and eat (of the fruits) thereof where you desire, but do not approach this tree, or you will both be among the wrongdoers"* (A'raf 7:19). Then, Satan began to whisper suggestions to them, bringing openly before their minds all their shame that had been hidden from them before:

> Then Satan made an evil suggestion to both of them that he might reveal to them their private parts that had remained hidden from them (and waken their carnal impulses), and he said, "Your Lord has forbidden you this tree only lest you should become sovereigns, or lest you should become immortals." (A'raf 7:20)

What harm was Adam causing to anyone? He was dwelling in the Garden, observing the manifestations of the Most Beautiful Names of God in contentment and gratification. However, his submission and acquiescence and the total tranquil obedience which he displayed toward his Lord added more fuel to Satan's rage. Was Adam not the cause of his expulsion? Revenge was sweet and Adam had to be punished accordingly. This is why Satan searched constantly for a weakness in Adam, and he found it. God Almighty had shown a tree to Adam and his partner and said, *"Do not approach it."* In fact, approaching this tree was part of Adam's nature. It was the only way that the tree of Adam's future generations would blossom. Yet, he was confronted with a test, and he had to obey the commandment of his Lord. Finally, Satan's devious trickery worked, and Adam reached out to the forbidden tree. However, this period of blunder did not last, and Adam repented. Feeling regret, he quickly regained his composure and submitted to his Lord:

> Adam received from his Lord words that he perceived to be inspired in him (because of his remorse, and he pleaded through them for God's forgiveness). In return He accepted his repentance. He is the One Who accepts repentance and returns it

with liberal forgiveness and additional reward, the All-Compassionate. (Baqara 2:37)

Adam pleaded with his Lord to teach him what to say so that he might be forgiven. He desired to knock on the door of mercy so that once again he could enter His exalted presence. Adam's sincere submission and repentance brought heavenly mercy. His Lord accepted his contrition. A hadith explains, "When you repent and ask for His forgiveness it will be regarded as if you had never committed that sin."[29] This means that from this point on, it would be wrong to assign a lapse to Adam, since he offered the most acceptable of atonement, and it would be indecent to ascribe a sin to Adam, the *Safiyu'llah* ('the Chosen of God').

Unlike Adam, who turned to his Lord and atoned, Satan stubbornly refused and continued his revolt. This is the difference between those who make an error and those who willfully rebel. On one side, there is a soul in total submission even in the process of being expelled from Paradise. His future family tree will yield fruits such as the perfection of manner, Prophet Muhammad, and once again the children of Adam will begin their quest for Paradise. On the other side, the cursed soul of Satan is in constant descent. Every minute that passes by, he is falling further toward *gayya*, an abyss at the bottom of hell.[30]

There are various explanations regarding the tree that Adam and his partner were ordered to keep away from; some say it was a fig tree and others have suggested plants such as hyacinth, wine or wheat. However, there are no clear indications, neither in the Qur'an, nor in authentic hadith, as to the definition of this tree. Perhaps the Almighty mentions the 'forbidden tree' in a symbolic sense. All we have been informed is that it had the potential to obliterate Adam's serenity and happiness.[31]

The Qur'an explains that Adam and his partner approached the tree and *"when they tasted the tree, their private parts (and all the apparently shameful, evil impulses in their creation) were revealed to them, and both began to cover themselves with leaves from the Garden"*

(A'raf 7:22). Once they had disobeyed the commandment, they discovered something new about themselves which was already implanted in their nature. This series of events suggests that the metaphorical meaning of the 'tree' described by the revelations is nothing other than sexual interaction between Adam and his spouse. The fact of the matter is that human beings are created in pairs of male and female so that they can reproduce. At first God prevented them from discovering this impulse placed in their nature, but then He used it as a means of assessment.

All that is said about the issue—which inevitably caused the expulsion of Adam and Eve from the Garden—does not go further than mere speculation because God has not provided clear information revealing the meaning of this 'forbidden tree.' It is unnecessary to insist on the definition, since we will never be able to achieve a definite result. All we need to know is that Adam and his spouse encountered an attractive sensation which they had not felt before and this was their test. Although they had been cautioned about the forbidden tree, Satan succeeded in his devious plan to persuade them, and as a result they were subjected to a serious admonishment. However, as soon as they realized their mistake, they repented in humility and turned to their Lord for forgiveness. God, the Owner of Infinite Mercy accepted their sincere prayers and forgave them.

2

Satan as Mentioned in the
Qur'an and Hadith

SATAN DESCRIBED IN THE QUR'AN

The Qur'an is a book of guidance for humankind. It teaches them the way of life most appropriate to their nature. It encourages them to achieve this goal. It presents the path of salvation before them, elucidating the positives and negatives. The exalted words of God warn us against Satan, *"For Satan is a manifest enemy to humankind."*[1] This greatest adversary of humans possesses no sympathy. This is why God says, *"Surely, Satan is an enemy to you, so treat him as an enemy"* (Fatir 35:6). Thus, He draws our attention to the clear threat. Satan's most obvious trait is his declaration of war on humankind. He makes his intention quite obvious and states his strategy of attacking humankind: *"I will surely lie in wait for them on Your straight path. Then I will come upon them from before them and from behind them, and from their right and from their left. And You will not find most of them thankful"* (A'raf 7:16–17).

Satan targeted his weapons of destruction at humanity and willed to use all of his faculties to bring man down. From that point on, all his concerns have been focused on dragging humans into a life that contradicts their nature. He has closed himself to good, and everything related to good has totally perished from his nature. He will use all the evil abilities and strategies that he has developed in order to destroy humankind. In the course of attacking humanity, he observes no boundaries or limits. When he succeeds in manipulating a human being into committing an evil act, he does not quit. He will continue his campaign by whispering words of deception, using tactics of provocation, and also with insidious approaches and false promises he will drag the person to his path. He will remind the person of the most inappropriate things at the most unexpected places. He will never be satisfied, and so he will continue to increase the treatment until the person totally loses control.

When Satan gets people under his control, he makes them forget their morals, values and faith. He causes them to forget God, and he even tricks them into believing that he (Satan) does not exist. He directs them toward sins, and follows this with a rain of commands. Each command has the potential to take man further and further away from the right path because Satan commands nothing but evil.[2]

Satan works in various ways. Along with approaching individuals, he also works on groups and communities. The Qur'an reminds us of this with the following verses:

> O you who believe! Intoxicants, games of chance, sacrifices to (anything serving the function of) idols (and at places consecrated for offerings to other than God) and (the pagan practice of) divination by arrows (and similar practices) are a loathsome evil of Satan's doing; so turn wholly away from such (abomination) so that you may prosper (in both worlds). Satan only seeks to promote enmity and hatred among you by means of intoxicants and games of chance, and to bar you from the remembrance of God and from the Prayer. So, then, will you abstain? (Maeda 5:90–91)

Alcohol and gambling are diseases that paralyze individuals and society. Those who are addicted to these maladies will lead unhappy lives in proportion to their level of addiction. It is probable that they will also make those around them unhappy, and eventually lose their families because of their crumbling personalities and declining self-esteem. Society cannot expect any valuable input from these people.

One can only protect oneself from Satan's trickery by listening to the advice of the holy Qur'an: *And say to My servants that they should always speak (even when disputing with others) that which is the best. Satan is ever ready to sow discord among them. For Satan indeed is a manifest enemy for humankind* (Isra 17:53). Being kind to others by abstaining from saying bad words and choosing carefully the things we say to others will defeat Satan's plan to destroy harmony, so it plays a great role in the continuation of peace among people. The holy Qur'an draws our attention to this important issue:

> O you who believe! Come in full submission to God, all of you (without allowing any discord among you due to worldly reasons), and do not follow in the footsteps of Satan, for indeed he is a manifest enemy to you (seeking to seduce you to rebel against God with glittering promises). (Baqara 2:208)

This verse informs us that Satan is out to divide society and peace is the only means of defense; otherwise, humankind will be following in the footsteps of Satan.

Furthermore, Satan transforms his followers into indecent, licentious beings:

> O you who believe! Do not follow in the footsteps of Satan. Whoever follows in the footsteps of Satan, (let him know well that) Satan insistently calls to all that is indecent and shameful, and all that is evil. Were it not for God's bounty on you, and His mercy, not one of you would have ever attained purity; but God purifies whomever He wills. God is All-Hearing, All-Knowing. (Nur 24:21)

The Qur'an addresses the whole of humankind, regardless of whether they are believers or not, and invites people to consume what is right. It asks humans to refrain from filthy food, what is the right of others and doubtful things by consuming clean and lawful products. The warning is that if we do not follow these guidelines, we will be entering Satan's zone of despondency, since Satan continuously works on our minds, insidiously entering into our blood vessels, ordering us to act in the name of all that is evil and indecent:

> O humankind! (Observe what God commands you. He has made you dwell on the earth, so) eat of what is on the earth provided it is lawful, pure and wholesome (in composition and religiously); and do not follow in the footsteps of Satan (who deceives both those who are followed and those who follow);

indeed he is a manifest enemy to you. He only commands you to evil and indecency and that you should speak against God the things about which you have no (sure) knowledge. (Baqara 2:168–169)

On the Day of Judgment, the Almighty Creator will address the sinners:

And you, O disbelieving criminals! Get you apart this Day! Did I not make a covenant with you, O children of Adam, that you should not worship Satan – indeed he is a manifest enemy to you – and that you should worship Me alone? This is a straight path (for you to follow). Yet he has assuredly caused great multitudes of you to go astray. Should you not reason and take heed? This is Hell with which you were threatened (repeatedly). (Ya.Sin 36:59–63)

Abraham, the forefather of prophets, used the same approach as he warned his polytheist father of a gloomy fate: *"O my father! Do not worship Satan (by obeying his suggestion to you to worship idols)! Satan is ever rebellious against the All-Merciful"* (Maryam 19:44). Abraham's father was not a Satan worshipper; he worshipped the idols of his tribe. Hence, his father replied to Abraham, *"Have you turned away from my deities, O Abraham?"* (Maryam 19:46). Abraham knew this, and on one occasion he smashed all the idols but one and said to his father, *"Oh dear father, do not worship Satan."* He was implying that worshipping anything other than God was the same as worshipping Satan. Abraham classified his tribe's idolatry as worshipping Satan.

His view is supported by the following verse from the Qur'an: *"In His stead they invoke female deities—(in so doing) they in fact invoke none but a haughty, rebellious Satan"* (Nisa 4:117). All those worshipped other than God are termed *taghut* by the holy Qur'an.

In one of his prayers, Prophet Job cried to his Lord, *"Surely Satan has caused me to be afflicted with distress and great suffering!"* (Sad 38:41). The affliction described in the verse is translated as Satan finding a way to whisper into the heart.[3]

Prophet Solomon and black magic

The book of our Lord mentions Satan in the verses regarding Solomon. During the time of Solomon, satans would frequently eavesdrop on heavenly knowledge and add lies to the information they had learned before passing it over to the diviner magicians of that era. The few facts which were distributed among all the lies would encourage magicians to believe Satan. They would repeat everything they had learnt from him. In time, these magicians recorded everything they had been taught. The information in these books eventually entered into stories and novels, and they were used with evil intent.

During his reign, Prophet Solomon ordered the collection of all these books, and then he buried them in a vault underneath his throne. Following Solomon's death, a human satan dug up the books. Rumors began to spread about Solomon's wealth. People claimed that Solomon had acquired all of his treasures by using magic. These evil allegations spread like a disease. People began to believe that Solomon was a magician:[4] *"And (just as their ancestors did) they follow the fictions the satans invented and spread about the rule of Solomon (falsely attributing his employment of the jinn, devils, and animals in his kingdom to sorcery)"* (Baqara 2:102). The verse clearly points out the satanic behavior.

The Jews regarded Solomon as a magician. Later, when the Qur'an elucidated the issue, they became enemies of Gabriel, and they refused to accept Muhammad as the Messenger of God. They would stubbornly repeat the fabrication that Solomon was not a Prophet as Muhammad declared but a magician. According to their claim, Solomon must have been an unbeliever—God forgive us for the expression—because casting spells to harm others is rebellion against God.[5]

In defense of Solomon, the Qur'an illuminates the issue by stating that he was a Prophet of God, not a magician. He was certainly not an unbeliever. On the contrary, those who claimed that he was a magician and used black magic to harm others are the real unbe-lievers: *"But (ascribing creativity or creative effect to sorcery is a kind of unbelief and) Solomon (being a Prophet and excellent servant of God) never disbelieved. Rather, the satans (who spread false things about his rule) disbelieved, teaching people sorcery"* (Baqara 2:102). In this verse, 'satans' indicates human and jinn satans. When these species per-form satanic functions and behave like Satan, they become the same as Satan. The meaning of the Qur'anic quotation above clearly sug-gests this.[6]

Prophet Solomon prayed to God, *"My Lord, forgive me, and bestow on me a kingdom which will not suit anyone after me. Surely You are the All-Bestowing"* (Sad 38:35). Almighty God accepted his prayer and granted his wish:

> We (accepted his prayer and) subdued the wind to his service,
> so that it coursed gently by his command wherever he willed;
> and of the satans (We made subservient to him) every builder
> (on earth) and diver (to extract precious stones from the sea)
> and others linked together in fetters. (Sad 38:36–38)

In the verse above the jinn that were under Solomon's sover-eignty are referred to as satans. The following verse in Sura Saba clearly specifies them as jinn:

> Among the jinn were some who, by the leave of his Lord,
> worked under him. Whoever of them swerved away from Our
> command (by disobeying him), We would make him taste the
> punishment of a fiery blaze. They made for him whatever he
> wished—sanctuaries, and figures (of inanimate objects), and
> carvings, as well as basins like ponds and boilers built into the
> ground. (Saba 34:12–13)

We cannot even imagine a situation where jinn that were believers would disobey a Prophet. For this reason, there would be no need for them to be threatened with fire. So such a warning must have been issued to those who could possibly have disobeyed Solomon, and this means they were the evil ones among the jinn who did not believe. In the above verse, the Qur'an describes them as the satanic jinn.

Spying

On earth, satans constantly work in the name of wickedness, and they never give up their attempts to ascend to heavens to spy on angels. Their aim is to collect valuable information which they can deliver to human beings with satanic attributes. Their goal is to quicken the process of chaos and mischief on earth. While spying on the angels for their evil mission, those satans who are able to obtain something from the angels are hit with a fiery object. The Qur'an explains their venture:

> We have indeed adorned the lowest heaven (the heaven of the world) with an ornament—the stars, (for beauty) and for guard against every devil persistent in haughty rebellion. They cannot hear anything from the High Assembly (of the angels of the heavens)—and (whenever they attempt to hear) become targets of missiles from all directions, repelled, and for them is a perpetual punishment—excepting one who snatches something by stealth, and is pursued (and destroyed) by a piercing shooting star. (Saffat 37:6–10)

In the pre-Islamic era, those evil ones would frequently spy on angels; however, they could not continue to perform their evil work after the revelation of the Qur'an had begun. Satan and his aids admit this reality:

> But now when we sought to reach heaven, we found it filled with stern guards and flaming fires (shooting stars). We used to be established in position to overhear (its inhabitants); but now whoever attempts to listen finds a flaming fire in wait for him. (Jinn 72:8–9)

Some commentators suggested that the 'flaming fires' are to be taken literally.[7] They believe that the satans who attempt to eavesdrop on angels are punished with objects such as meteorites. However, the late Islamic scholar Elmalılı Hamdi Yazır insists that the word 'flaming fires' is metaphorical: "It would be more appropriate to think of a meaning along the lines of the light of Prophethood and the powerful rays of truth emitted from the holy Qur'an acting as a defense mechanism against these superstitious ideologies. It is our conclusion that the words carry a deeper meaning."[8] Only God knows the whole truth.

The Qur'an takes the matter of eavesdropping seriously. Only God knows, perhaps it is to form a barrier and to prevent the emergence of rumors that may accuse Prophet Muhammad of being a diviner and the Qur'an of being a book of divination. This assumption is based on the fact that before Prophet Muhammad's time people believed that soothsayers possessed the ability to foretell the future. In the pre-Islamic era, soothsaying or fortune-telling was very widespread among the Arabs as well. There was a possibility that the Arabs might relate their superstitions to the verses revealed in the holy Qur'an, once the Prophet began to recite them. So, God stated in the Qur'an, "*So (O Messenger, continue to) preach and remind; by God's grace, you are not a soothsayer, nor a madman*" (Tur 52:29) and, "*Nor is it (the Qur'an) a soothsayer's speech (pretending to foretell events). How little is it that you reflect and be mindful! (No indeed!) It is a Revelation being sent down in parts from the Lord of the worlds*" (Haqqa 69:42–43). God prevented the spread of rumors and delusion with these verses. As a dimension of His infinite mercy, God draws attention to the Qur'an over and over again: "*It is not the satans who have brought down this (Book). It is neither (permitted nor proper) for them, nor is it within their power (to do that)*" (Shuara 26:210–211). Also, we are informed that satans descend upon calumniators and these sinners use their lies to deceive others. The noble Prophet and the holy Message he conveyed have been defended by Almighty God.

Along with being a guide to humanity, the holy Qur'an is also God's mercy. This holy Book manifests its attribute of guidance by providing information in relation to Satan and demonstrates its mercy by coaching humanity with strategies for self-protection. The Qur'an reminds us of the urgency of this issue:

> And if a prompting from Satan should cause you hurt (as you carry out your mission or during worship or in your everyday life), seek refuge in God. He is All-Hearing, All-Knowing. Those who keep from disobedience to God in reverence for Him and piety—when a suggestion from Satan touches them, they are alert and remember God, and then they have clear discernment. Whereas their brothers (the brothers of the satans in the form of human beings)—satans draw them deeper into error and do not relax in their efforts. (A'raf 7:200–202)

Living life as one pleases increases Satan's power of influence on man. Human and jinn devils always stand close to those who willfully ignore remembrance of God:

> Whoever willfully ignores the remembrance of the All-Merciful (and lives as if He did not exist always watching him), We assign to him a devil, who becomes his closest comrade. Such devils certainly bar them from the way (of truth). Yet they think (in themselves) that they are rightly guided. (Zukhruf 43:36–37)

Using intoxicants

Satan uses various tactics to drive humankind into deviation. Intoxicants are one of his favorite tools. He uses them to draw human beings into an ambiance God is not pleased with. We are encouraged to focus our attention on this important issue in the Qur'an: "*Satan only hopes to provoke enmity and hatred among you by means of intoxicants and games of chance, and to bar you from the remembrance of God and from the Prayer. So, then, will you abstain?*" (Maeda 5:91).

These filthy habits are used by Iblis to erode the social structure. The broken families, inhumane incidents, and abundance of ghastly occurrences which paralyze society clearly show the gruesome results of alcohol consumption. It is obvious that those under the influence of intoxicants lose control to a certain extent, and they are more likely to behave in an antisocial manner. There is a strong connection between alcohol consumption and Satan simply because intoxicants make people more vulnerable to his attacks. For this reason, there is a warning following the establishment of a connection between Satan and alcohol consumption.

The following story illustrates what follows alcohol consumption: "There was a pious man who would retreat to his corner worshiping God in total obedience. A woman desired him, so she sent her servant over requesting him to testify on a certain matter. As the man entered her house, she locked the door behind him and said, 'I did not call you to be a witness. I want you to choose one of the following options; kill this child, sleep with me or drink some wine. If you refuse, I will bring shame to your name.' The man thought to himself, 'Alcohol is the best option so I have to choose drinking.' The man drank and became intoxicated. Then, he killed the child and slept with the woman."[9]

Alcohol consumption causes a negative change in the atmosphere, harming not only the offender but also others within the same milieu. Abu Hurayra explains, "One day a drunken man was brought before the Messenger of God. We began to strike him with our hands, shoes and garments. Suddenly, a man from the crowd shouted insults at him, 'Shame on you! May God condemn you!' Upon hearing this, the noble Prophet said, 'Do not aid Satan by testifying against your brother.'" According to another narrator, the noble Prophet said, "Do not curse him, for I swear by the Almighty that he loves God and His Messenger."[10] Bukhari does not provide the name of the person who failed to control his temper and cursed his brother. Clearly, a wrongful act had given birth to another; temper is from Satan and it results in regret. This becomes quite apparent when we analyze the incident which occurred between the two sons of Adam:

Narrate to them (O Messenger) in truth the exemplary experience of the two sons of Adam, when they each offered a sacrifice, and it was accepted from one of them, and not accepted from the other. "I will surely kill you," said the one. "God accepts only from the sincere and truly pious," said the other. "Yet if you stretch out your hand against me to kill me, I will not stretch out my hand against you to kill you. Surely I fear God, the Lord of the worlds. (In refusing to fight you and remembering to fear God) I desire indeed (to warn you) that you will bear the burden of my sin (were I to take part in fighting you) and your own sin (for seeking to kill me) and so you will be among the companions of the Fire. For that is the recompense of wrongdoers." (This warning served only to fuel the other's passion.) His carnal, evil-commanding soul prompted him to kill his brother, and he killed him, thus becoming among the losers. (He did not know what to do with the dead body of his brother.) Then God sent forth a raven, scratching in the earth, to show him how he might cover the corpse of his brother. So seeing, he cried, "Oh, alas for me! Am I then unable even to be like this raven, and so find a way to cover the corpse of my brother?" And he became distraught with remorse. (Maeda 5:27–31)

Whispers

The Qur'an uses the word *najwa* when it is referring to 'talks in secret, whispers and rumors'[11]: "*Secret counsels are only (a provocation) from Satan, in order that he may cause grief to the believers; yet he cannot harm them in anything unless by God's leave; and in God let the believers put their trust*" (Mujadila 58:10). *Najwa* is a secret shared by two persons. It is also defined as a secret conversation between people. Although it is usually identified as a secret conversation, it may also occur out in the open.[12] Believers are prohibited from *najwa*. Committing sins, violating the rights of others and talking behind the Prophet's back have been forbidden by God:

O you who believe! If you hold secret counsels, do not hold secret counsels to commit sins, or for (urging one another to) offensiveness and disobedience to the Messenger; but rather

> hold counsels for godliness, righteousness, and piety. Keep
> from disobedience to God in reverence for Him, and piety, to
> Whom you will be gathered. (Mujadila 58:9)

Also, the noble Prophet stated, "When three of you get together, let two of you not speak in secret because this will offend the other."[13] There is no doubt that secret talks between two people will bring discomfort to the third, causing him to have negative thoughts about the other two. This type of behavior will also damage the structure of society. Scholars have concluded that two people speaking in a language next to a third person who does not understand is the same as the whispers of Satan.[14]

Other issues

As an analogy the holy Qur'an likens all evil behavior to satans. There are, however, other comparisons such as Satan's siblings, Satan's companions and Satan's party. When wasting became forbidden, those who waste were likened to Satan's siblings.[15] As the Qur'an instructs believers to struggle against those who embrace entities other than God, those people are defined as Satan's companions. The verse also states that their tools of deception, traps and trickery are weak. Those who become total slaves of Satan are defined as members of Satan's party.

When the Qur'an forbids the committing of some acts, it relates them to Satan:

> O you who believe! Intoxicants, games of chance, sacrifices to
> (anything serving the function of) idols (and at places conse-
> crated for offerings to other than God) and (the pagan practice
> of) divination by arrows (and similar practices) are a loath-
> some evil of Satan's doing; so turn wholly away from it so that
> you may prosper (in both worlds). (Maeda 5:90)

Once people fall into these traps, there is no way of stopping sins from being committed. All type of atrocities will be committed, and thus religion and the Day of Judgment will be forgotten.[16]

What is expected of humans is to be prepared against this unforgiving enemy by living a life in which they seek only to please God.

SATAN DESCRIBED IN THE HADITH

Hadiths are defined as Prophet Muhammad's words, acts, and confirmations.[17] The noble Prophet, peace and blessings be upon him, sometimes delivered verbal information regarding an issue and at times taught people with his actions. There were also times when he approved of an act displayed next to him by keeping silent. These are all forms of hadith and, along with the Qur'an, they show Muslims the way of pleasing God. The Qur'an is the most beautiful of all words and God's Messenger is the best of all guides.[18] His guidance manifests in his words, and it is demonstrated by his behavior. Practicing what he preached was the best evidence pointing to the magnitude of his quality as a guide.

Whenever it was necessary, he would open the topic of Satan, presenting strategies of defense and emphasizing the importance of seeking refuge in God from the evil one. Now, we shall study Satan as described by the noble Prophet in the hadith. In doing so, we shall attempt to understand the Prophet's perception of Satan.

Dwelling in the bloodstream

As expressed in the Qur'an, Satan found his conjecture about humankind true: *"Iblis certainly found his conjecture (about humankind) true in what they did. (He called them and) they followed him, all but a group of true believers"* (Saba 34:20). Concerning his conjecture about humankind, Satan said,

> "My Lord! Because You have allowed me to rebel and go astray, I will indeed deck out to be appealing to them on the earth (the worldly, material dimension of human existence and the path of error), and I will surely cause them all to rebel and go astray, except Your servants from among them, endowed with sincerity in faith and Your worship." (Hijr 15:39–40)

Satan succeeded in his claim and except for a group of sincere believers, they have all followed in his footsteps.

The Prophet's wife Safiyya explains the dwelling of Satan in the human blood vessels: "The Messenger of God had gone away on a retreat. I went to visit him one night. We spoke for awhile then I got up to return home. (Safiyya lived next door to Usama and they stood in front of the Masjid.) Two people were passing by. When they saw the Prophet, they quickened their steps. The noble Prophet shouted, 'Stay where you are!' Then he said, 'This is my wife Safiyya bint Huyay.' They replied, 'Glory be to God, O God's Messenger!' The Prophet explained, 'Satan dwells in the bloodstream; I feared that he may plant bad thoughts in your heart.'"[19]

Scholars such as Qadi Iyad took the hadith literally and suggested that God gave Satan the ability to travel through the bloodstreams of human beings. However, others interpreted it differently, arguing that the hadith refers to Satan's capacity for deception through whispers. This suggests that Satan is like blood to a human; he never leaves his side.[20] This hadith, which is narrated in different versions, provides a fair understanding of Satan's abilities.

Entering the human body

Some hadiths suggest that Satan also has the ability of possession. In a hadith transmitted by Abu Hurayra, the noble Prophet stated, "If you wake up in the middle of the night, you should blow your nose three times, since Satan rests in the nasal passages."[21] The Arabic word *khayshum* used to describe the nasal passages in the hadith also has the meanings of the top part of the nose, the entire nose, and an area located in the deeper part of the nose, close to the brain. The interpretations are quite similar and it suggests that Satan uses the nasal openings to enter the human body.

Scholars who concur with Qadi Iyad say that the words of the Messenger of God are reality. The reason for this is that the nasal holes are gateways to the body which open up to the heart. Other than the nasal and ear holes, there are no other holes in the human body which constantly remain open. Hence, Satan cannot open what is closed.[22] Imam Nawawi believes the hadith is metaphorical and he interprets it thus: "Throughout the day, humidity, dust, and germs enter the body through the nasal passages; this in turn causes a health risk."[23]

Another place where Satan dwells is the gap between fingernails and flesh. The noble Prophet stated, "Comb your beards with fingers and trim your fingernails because Satan likes to dwell between your flesh and fingernails."[24] This hadith could also be interpreted in the same way as the previous one because long fingernails gather filth and germs and also affect the appearance in a negative way.

Another issue that may be considered in the same category is yawning. The noble Prophet said, "Yawning is from Satan; if any of you gets the urge to yawn, he should attempt to swallow it to the best of his ability."[25] Another hadith suggests that the mouth should be covered during a yawn.[26] In general, yawning is a sign of laziness or indolence. Perhaps it was related to Satan because he is fond of laziness and lazy people. In contrast to sneezing, yawning is a sign of heaviness in the body, fullness of the tummy and languor. It is an indication of leaning toward idleness. These are all tools which Satan uses to defeat humankind.

Utilizing wrath

Wrath means 'anger, rage or fury.'[27] In normal conditions, human beings hold their emotions in balance, and in essence they are distant from sins. Conversely, Satan possesses the ability to draw them into his atmosphere, causing them to act in contradiction to their nature. In a short-lived period of rage, those who cannot control their temper lose their balance and act in an inappropriate manner.

Anger is an emotion planted in our souls, and every human being possesses it on different levels. In life, one does not always find the medium one prefers. Sometimes, the words or actions of others displease us. Hence, this may trigger the emotion of anger. This is quite normal to a certain extent. If it was not regarded as normal behavior, the noble Prophet would never have displayed anger. In fact, what is expected of human beings is to control and manage anger. It would be illogical to anticipate that one should never get angry. Controlling one's temper can significantly change the result. "Losing control of common sense during anger may result in profanity, brawls and many other regrettable acts which are forbidden by God. In some cases uncontrollable bursts of rage can make murderers out of people, transforming them into miserable beings for the rest of their lives. The result of an uncontrollable rage is nothing other than regret which bears no significance anymore."[28] So, anger is not absolutely opposed; when it is controlled with patience, it can even earn rewards. When the Qur'an explains the attributes of those who possess *taqwa* (piety), it describes them as those who, *"spend (out of whatever God has provided for them) both in ease. and hardship, ever-restraining their rage (even when provoked and able to retaliate), and pardoning people (their offenses). God loves (such) people who are devoted to doing good, aware that God is seeing them."* (Imran 3:134). The Prophet stated, "Being a wrestler is not a sign of strength; true strength is possessed by those who control their anger."[29]

There were times when even the Prophet displayed anger. But on each occasion he preferred to please God and acted in a sensible manner, being a role model for all of us. Shakek explains, "One day, God's Messenger was distributing the spoils of war. A man from the Helpers said, 'The distribution is not fair.' I replied, 'I swear by Almighty God, I will tell this to the noble Messenger.' I walked over to the Prophet. There were people standing near him, so I spoke softly to his ear and explained what the person had claimed. The Messenger was upset as his face turned red. Then, he said, 'May God have mercy on Moses, he endured much more than I and showed patience.'"[30] Sulayman ibn Surad narrates "Two men disputed in the presence of the Prophet while we were sitting with him. One of the two was so upset that his face had turned red. The noble Messenger said, 'I know a word that if he recites it, what he feels will go away: *A'udhu bi'llahi min ash-shaytani'r-rajim* (I seek refuge in God from Satan eternally rejected [from God's Mercy]).' When they said to the man, 'Do you not hear what God's Messenger is saying?' he replied, 'I am not insane.'"

It is said that "whoever defeats his rage will have triumph over his rivals, their satan and his own satan."[31] The period of anger carries the potential of falling into the path of Satan. Those who defeat their anger may at first seem to concede defeat, but in actuality they have turned the situation in their favor by showing patience and earning rewards from God.

Interacting with every newborn

Human beings possess an intricate structure. We are equipped with complexity. We have been gifted with a variety of physical and metaphysical mechanisms. Just as we have a close involvement with the present, we are also connected to the past and future. Satan is aware of all these; thus, he seeks to reach as far as the human hand does. If he fails to bring man down in one stage, he will attempt to do so in another. He will sit on the true path of God to blockade our way. The Qur'an gives Satan's own words:

> Now that You have allowed me to rebel and go astray, I will surely lie in wait for them on Your Straight Path (to lure them from it). Then I will come upon them from before them and from behind them, and from their right and from their left. And You will not find most of them thankful. (A'raf 7:16–17)

Satan does not waste any time before putting his plans into practice. He wishes to begin his work even before a human being's conception or at an embryonic stage. This is why the Messenger of God recommends, "Before you approach your wives, say, 'O Lord! Keep Satan away from us and from what you will grant.'"[32] Satan's evil work begins at the time of intercourse. This is the time when a suitable atmosphere has been established for him to begin his operation. If we fail to form an initial shield at the beginning, his evil will travel through the parents, affecting the newcomer. Consequently, he has the potential to influence human beings at an embryonic stage.[33]

Abu Hurayra explains, "There is no child whom Satan fails to interact with during birth. The cries of the newborn occur due to this interaction. The only people excluded from this interaction are Jesus and his mother."[34] After transmitting this hadith, Abu Hurayra added, "You may recite the following verse, *"I commend her and her offspring to You for protection from Satan eternally rejected (from God's Mercy)"* (Imran 3:36). When Mary's mother fell pregnant with her, she offered this prayer. Qadi Iyad said that this unique gift granted to Jesus and Mary was also valid for all Prophets.[35] It is obvious that one (Satan) who has failed to interact with Jesus and Mary can never have done so with the noble Messenger.

Satan's horns

In some hadiths, the Messenger of God uses the phrase, "Satan's horns." When we scrutinize these hadiths, we realize that this phrase is used with two different meanings. In the first group of hadiths it is used in relation to not performing prayers during sunrise and sunset. It is *makruh* (reprehensible) to perform prayers during these two periods. These hadiths tell us that the Morning Prayer should not be squeezed into a time when the sun is about to rise and the Afternoon Prayer should not be left to a time when the sun is setting. Regarding performing the Afternoon Prayer during sunset, the noble Messenger said, "This is the prayer of a hypocrite. He sits and observes the sun. As the sun appears between the horns of Satan, he stands up to pray. Then, he prays the four *raqat*s like a bird feeding on grain. He seldom remembers God."[36] With this statement, the Prophet forbids postponing prayers because of mere laziness and without any excuse.

Amr ibn Abasa relates a conversation with the Prophet: "I asked him, 'O Messenger of God, do you recognize me?' He replied, 'Yes, I spoke to you in Mecca.' Then, I asked him, 'O Messenger of God, can you teach me things that I do not know, what God has taught you, in particular regarding the Prayers?' The noble Messenger replied, 'Perform your Morning Prayer and then cease praying during sunrise, because the sun rises between the horns of Satan. This is the time when unbelievers worship the sun. Once the period of sunrise is completed, continue with your Prayers. The Prayer is proven and witnessed. Continue to perform it until the shadow of the spear becomes straight. Then, cease your Prayer because this is the time when hellfire becomes intense. Once the shadow appears again, continue praying until the time of the Afternoon Prayer. After performing the Afternoon Prayer, stop and do not pray until the sun fully sets, because the sun sets between the horns of Satan. This is when the unbelievers worship the sun.'"[37] In another hadith, the Messenger said, "Do not look for sunrise or sunset to pray because the sun rises between the horns of Satan."[38]

Satan's horns are interpreted as his power, strength and those who follow his path. Muhyiddin Nawawi approaches the hadith literally and says that during sunrise and sunset, Satan places his head in front of it, and thus those who pray during these periods worship him. This way Satan gets the chance to manipulate their minds.[39] The other interpretation regarding the phrase "Satan's horn" is a great sedition given birth in the East. Abdullah ibn Umar said, "I have witnessed the Prophet pointing to the East and saying, 'Sedition is there, and it will rise from the point of Satan's horns.'"[40] One time, the noble Prophet prayed, "O Lord, bless our Damascus and Yemen." The Companions said, "O Messenger of God, include Najd in your prayer." They repeated their request a few times. Then the noble Messenger said, "All sedition and instigations begin from there; it is where the horn of Satan emerges."[41]

On another occasion, the noble Prophet stood up in the Masjid, pointing toward the direction where Aisha's room was located, and stated, "That is where sedition is, the birth place of Satan's horns."[42] The Prophet's wives lived in rooms that had doors opening to the Masjid. The Prophet pointed his finger toward Aisha's room, which was located on the eastern side of the Masjid, suggesting that the sedition would begin from the East, where the people were unbelievers. In this way, he had miraculously informed people that seditions would begin from there. Indeed, as he had suggested, the incidents of Jamal and Siffin were triggered from the East. Also the emergence of the Kharijites occurred in Najd, a region located east of Medina.[43] The historic Mongol invasion and the rise of Communism in the twentieth century also emerged in the East. All of these occurrences are evidence of the Prophet's miraculous foresight.

Satan's involvement in food consumption

Some hadiths give the notion that like human beings, Satan also consumes food. In one hadith, God's Messenger says, "Do not eat or drink using your left hand because Satan eats and drinks with his left."[44] This hadith implies that Satan also consumes food and in doing so, he uses his left hand.

One of the Prophet's Companions, Umayya relates an incident, "One day, a man was eating next to God's Messenger. He had forgotten to recite *basmala* until the last few morsels. Then he stopped and said, *"Bismillah* for the beginning and the end." Upon hearing this, the noble Messenger smiled and said, 'Satan was eating with him. But when he recited the name of God, he (Satan) vomited all he had consumed.'"[45]

Abu Hudayfa explains, "When we dined with God's Messenger, we would not reach for food until he began. One day, as we were about to eat, a little girl came and attempted to grab a handful. The Messenger of God grabbed her hand. Then, a Bedouin tried the same thing. The noble Messenger grabbed his hand as well. Then, he said, 'If you do not say *basmala* at the beginning, you are allowing Satan to eat with you. Satan walked in with the little girl, and I grabbed her hand. Then, he joined the Bedouin and I grabbed his hand as well. I swear by Almighty God, Who has my soul in His possession, that I was holding the hand of Satan along with theirs."[46]

In relation to the issue emphasized in the last hadith, the noble Prophet states, "Satan never leaves your side, even when you are eating. If you drop a crumb on the floor, pick it up, clean it, and then eat it. Do not leave anything for Satan. Do not leave any food on your plate because one does not know which part of the meal is blessed."[47]

The creation and life of Satan is quite different from that of humankind. He experiences a life beyond the dimensions of our life. Even if he consumes food, we can be sure that it does not occur in the way we understand it. It is not right to assume that Satan uses his hands in the same way that we do. The noble Prophet is describing the significance of reciting the name of God before we begin to eat and advising people to eat with their right hand. Thus, he is illustrating the unpleasantness of skipping *basmala* and eating with the left hand, with an analogy.

His influence in dreams

Dreams are what one observes during sleep.[48] In the hadith another word is used, that is, *hulm*. The word *hulm* has the same meaning as dream, with a delicate distinction; all the good and blessed things observed during sleep are defined as dreams and all evil and ugliness experienced are defined as *hulm* (for example, nightmares and wet dreams). The noble Prophet makes this distinction by stating, "Dreams are from God and *hulm* is from Satan. If any of you experiences a bad dream, he should spit three times to his left and seek refuge in God. By doing this, he shall be protected from the nightmare."[49] In another version of the hadith, the Prophet states, "When one of you sees a good dream, he should feel happy. He should not report it except to those whom he loves."[50] As for the visions emanating from the devil, the Prophet said, "Those who experience *hulm* should not tell anyone about Satan's games played on them during their sleep."[51]

There are many types of dreams. The first one occurs directly by the instructions of God or angels, so this is an authentic dream. The second type of dream is satanic. These occur because of the hidden influence of Satan. His fabrications and deception transform into a product of imagination where the viewer observes evil things.[52] The third type of dream is when people are affected by their daily affairs and these incidents become embedded in their subconscious. Then, they are released during sleep as dreams. In relation to this issue, the noble Prophet stated, "When the time draws near (i.e., near the end of the world), the dream of a believer can hardly be false. And the truest vision will be of one who is himself the most truthful in speech. The vision of a Muslim is one part from forty-six parts of Prophethood,[53] and dreams are of three types. The first type is a good (authentic) dream which is a glad tiding from God; the second type causes distress and comes from Satan; and the third one is a suggestion of one's own mind. So, if any of you sees a dream which he does not like, he should get up and pray, and he should not relate it to anyone."[54]

There is no doubt that even satanic dreams which cause distress during sleep are created by God. They are related to Satan because of their nature. Associating all types of ugliness and evil with Satan is a manner frequently used by the Prophet. This is clearly observed in the hadith.

The noble Prophet explains that Satan cannot imitate him in dreams, "Whoever has dreamt of me has actually seen me, for Satan cannot appear in my shape."[55] There are different versions of this hadith, but the point is the same and it is that dreams that involve the manifestation of the Prophet are authentic and genuine. They are not *hulm*. The important thing here is that the person seen in the dream should match the description of the noble Messenger described in the *Shama'il* ('the characteristics of the Prophet'). His manifestation in the dream should match his appearance when he was a young man, middle aged or mature as he passed away.[56]

Behavior on a journey

Satan is also mentioned in the hadith related to traveling. The Messenger of God states, "Those who travel alone on their mounts are satans. Those who travel in pairs on their mounts are also satans. The group of at least three travelers on their mounts is the *jama'a* ('congregation')."[57] Satan invites those who travel alone, whispering all sorts of offers into their hearts. A lonely person is more vulnerable to Satan's whispers. Although loneliness disappears when there are two, the vulnerability does not decrease. However, when there are three in a group, with the help of God, they will not adapt to the ways of Satan.

There are other negatives about traveling alone. One could fall ill, have an accident or even be attacked. If one dies alone during a journey, there may be no one there to arrange a proper burial. Even if all of the above do not apply, one would not be performing one's prayers in congregation, and this alone is enough to serve Satan's objective.[58]

Circulation during nightfall

Another issue addressed by the hadith is Satan's activities during nightfall. Jabir ibn Abdullah relates, "Do not let your children and your livestock out after sunset and keep them indoors until the darkness of the night disappears. This is the period in which satans spread out in the environment."[59] Another hadith recommends, "Keep your children indoors after sundown, because that is the time satans begin to spread out. Close your doors with *basmala* because Satan cannot open closed doors. Place covers over your drinking water and food. Then, recite *basmala* and put out your lanterns."[60]

It is our perception that these hadiths add a spiritual dimension to our daily lives and activities. They are reminding us to remember and recite the exalted name of God whilst we perform our normal activities such as locking our doors and covering our food. By seeking refuge in God, we are also protected from the whispers of Satan. The following hadith Jabir ibn Abdullah relates from the Messenger also supports this view: "When a person walks into his house reciting *basmala* and eats his meal beginning with *basmala*, Satan says to his aids, 'There is no place for you to rest tonight and there is no food to eat.' If the person does not remember God as he enters his house and dines without *basmala*, Satan says to his aids, 'You have found a place to sleep and dine.'"[61] There are also many other hadith recommending us to begin everything we do with *basmala*.

Satans are not fond of light and brightness. On the contrary, they are irritated by light and believe that there is power in darkness. They feel more comfortable in the dark and begin to move freely after nightfall. The conception is that they become highly active during the night, approaching people with their devious whispers. The common phrase "there is evil in darkness" strengthens our argument.

Satan's fear of Umar

The Messenger of God stated that Satan was afraid of Umar. Sa'd ibn Abi Waqqas explains, "The Messenger of God was talking to a group of women from Quraysh when Umar asked for permission to enter. The women were speaking loudly and requesting some things from the Prophet. As soon as they heard Umar's voice, they all got up and ran behind the curtains. The Messenger of God was smiling. Umar said, 'May God always give you joy, O God's Messenger!' The Messenger of God replied, 'I was surprised at these women; as soon as they heard your voice, they panicked and ran behind the curtains.' Umar said, 'It is you whom they should really respect.' Then, he turned toward the women and said, 'O enemies of your own souls, do you respect me more than the Prophet?' The group of women replied, 'We fear you because you are a bad-tempered man.' Then, God's Messenger said to Umar, 'I swear by Almighty God that if Satan runs into you, he would surely change his route.'"[62]

A bondmaid was playing the tambourine next to the Messenger of God. As soon as she saw Umar approaching, she hid her tambourine. Upon seeing this, God's Messenger said, "Surely, even Satan is afraid of you. This bondmaid was still playing the tambourine when Abu Bakr, Ali, and Uthman arrived, but when she saw you coming, she hid the tambourine in fear."[63]

We could construe Satan's fear of Umar literally. It is possible that Satan is afraid of Umar's authoritative appearance, assuming that he may be harmed by Umar. Scholars such as Qadi Iyad surmised that it is metaphorical. According to these scholars, Satan fears Umar because of his honesty, righteousness and his resistance to Satan. After explaining the two views, Nawawi concludes that the first view is more plausible.[64] It is likely that these dictums about Umar were because of his dedication to justice and fairness, and they may also be related to his majestic appearance.

Other issues

The Prophet was a model of consistency and his life was a paradigm for humanity. No matter which episode of his life you scrutinize, you will observe captivating behavior or a mesmerizing statement.

- Another superb thing about him was the neatness and cleanliness of his clothing. He did not have many garments, but he used efficiently the ones he owned. Everyone admired him when he dressed up. He always combed his hair.[65] He frequently cleaned his teeth[66] and also encouraged others to do so.[67] He was very fond of scents.[68] As he acted in this manner, he also advised others to be like that. One day, a man with a messy beard and hair came to a meeting. The Messenger made a gesture indicating that he should tidy up before walking in. The man tidied up and then walked in. God's Messenger then said, "Isn't it better to be like this than to have a messy appearance like Satan?"[69]
- The Messenger of God was a very contented individual; there was no place for extravagance in his life. For exam-

ple, he was not keen on people buying unnecessary items for their homes. He said, "In a home, one bed is for the man, and the other is for the woman. The third bed is for a guest. However, the fourth one belongs to Satan."[70]

- The Messenger of God stipulated that haste was also a satanic attribute: "Thinking, planning and being organized is from God; haste is from Satan."[71] With this statement, the Prophet encourages us to be more cautious.

- Some hadiths related the voice of donkeys to Satan and the voice of roosters to angels: "When you hear the sound of a rooster in the middle of the night, ask for the blessing of God because the animal has seen an angel. Seek refuge in God upon hearing the voice of a donkey because (at that instant) the animal is seeing Satan."[72]

- In one hadith transmitted by Abu Hurayra, the Prophet stated, "Bells are the instruments of Satan."[73]

- The Messenger of God also mentioned Satan in relation to lamentation. Ummu Salama explains, "When my husband died, I decided to wail in a spectacular fashion for my spouse who had died in exile. A woman was going to join me in my lamentation. However, I stopped crying when the Messenger of God said, 'Are you going to invite Satan back into your house, when God has expelled him?'"[74]

- Hadith also suggest that it is inappropriate for men and women who are not family members or not married to each other to be alone with each other. "A male should not be alone with a female stranger (who is lawful for him in marriage); in such a situation the third person would be Satan."[75] The two sexes have been tested with each other since the beginning of history. Today this has become more apparent.

- The noble Messenger associated camels with Satan: "Do not perform your prayers in camel barns because camels are from Satan."[76] This phrase also indicates that by nature camels can harm humans.

- Also, it is said: "Black dogs are from Satan."[77] Black dogs seem to be more ferocious and vicious than others.

In conclusion, we can say that God's Messenger associates many things with Satan. When he talks about Satan, is he referring to Iblis, the evil one that refused to bow down before Adam and was expelled from Paradise? Or is he speaking about Satan's human and jinn aids on earth? Could it be that he is correlating all evil and ugly acts to Satan? All of these hadiths relating to Satan have been examined by scholars who have proposed various interpretations. No matter what the explanation is, one should be aware of Satan or Iblis. He is an evil to fear, so the noble Messenger cautions us through the hadith. What is expected of us is to be careful, so that we do not fall into Satan's evil web of deception.

3

Satan's Attributes, Methods and
Infestation of the Heart

ATTRIBUTES OF SATAN

Using his own free will, Satan eliminated all potential good which originally existed in his soul and developed only his abilities for evil. Since he filled his soul with rebellion, there was no room left for faith. Just as a man in a rage is full of hatred, the life of Satan is filled with evil. In fact, he has become one with evil and has the potential to commit all types of malevolence.

The significant attributes and functions of Satan are:

Antagonism

Satan's enmity toward human beings is obvious. He has declared war on Adam and his descendants who caused his hidden feelings of rebellion and revolt to surface. In total disrespect he said to God: *"'Shall I prostrate myself before one whom You created of clay?' He said, 'Do You see this that You have honored above me? Indeed, if You grant me respite till the Day of Resurrection, I will certainly bring his descendants under my sway, all but a few!'"* (Isra 17:61–62)

Almighty God informed us of Satan's hostility and instructed us also to regard him as our enemy: *"Surely Satan is an enemy to you, so treat him as an enemy (do not follow him, and be alert against him). He calls his party (of followers) but that they may become companions of the Blaze"* (Fatr 35:6). It is imperative that we acknowledge his hostility so that we may prepare ourselves. Whether he is recognized as an archenemy or not, those who follow his path will be led to a blazing inferno, since he will never rest until he witnesses the demise of humanity.

His first action was to sway Adam and his wife from the straight path:

> Then Satan made an evil suggestion to both of them that he
> might reveal to them their private parts that had remained hid-
> den from them (and waken their carnal impulses), and he said,
> "Your Lord has forbidden you this tree only lest you should
> become sovereigns or lest you should become immortals." And
> he swore to them, "Truly, I am for you a sincere adviser." Thus
> he led them on by delusion; and when they tasted the tree, their
> private parts (and all the apparently shameful, evil impulses in
> their creation) were revealed to them, and both began to cover
> themselves with leaves from the Garden. (A'raf 7:20–22)

Satan deceived both of them. "Adam and Eve thought that no
one would testify falsely before God; they were misled."[1]

Whilst Adam and his partner were feeling ashamed of what
they had done, they were reprimanded: *"And their Lord called out
to them, 'Did I not prohibit you from that tree, and did I not say to you
that Satan is a manifest enemy to you?'"* (A'raf 7:22).Yet, they had
been warned earlier, *"O Adam, surely this is an enemy to you and
your wife; so let him not drive the two of you out of the Garden, lest you
become distressed"* (Ta Ha 20:117). When they were later reminded
about that warning, in humility, they replied, *"Our Lord! We have
wronged ourselves, and if You do not forgive us and do not have mercy
on us, we will surely be among those who have lost!"* (A'raf 7:23) They
realized their mistake, so they confessed and repented.

If we compare the answers given by Iblis and Adam we will
realize the blessing of the words which were inspired in the hearts of
Adam and Eve. This in turn signifies the great distinction between
Adam and Iblis and manifests the magnitude of Iblis' ignorance in
comparing earth to fire.[2]

Satan displayed his hostility in his initial deception by lying,
manipulating and falsely testifying by the name of God. Then, he
ignobly left the scene. God reminds us of this incident so that we
may protect ourselves from falling into the same trap:

> O children of Adam! Never let Satan seduce you (and cause
> you to fail in similar trials) as he caused your (ancestral) par-
> ents to be driven out of the Garden, pulling off from them

their garment and revealing to them their private parts (and the carnal impulses ingrained in them). He sees you, he and his host (see you), from where you do not see them. We have made satans the confidants and fellow-criminals of those who do not believe. (A'raf 7:27)

Satan's enmity is his foremost attribute. All of his other attributes are there to support this particular one. As will be explained in detail later, Satan approaches by stealth, he deceives and misleads. He whispers, decorates, threatens, makes false promises, instigates, and sets unimaginable traps. He does all these because he has sworn vengeance against humankind.

Although he cannot be observed, he cunningly enters our blood vessels, drawing closer to the heart. He commands us to commit disgraceful acts that displease God. What the phrase 'he commands' implies is that he decorates evil acts, and then throws them into our imagination, encouraging us to sin. The term 'command' is used figuratively to illustrate the vileness of following in his footsteps.[3] It may also suggest that those who follow his path have chosen him as their leader. Satan presents bad as good, lies as truth, and evil as blessing. He misleads people by showing unlawful as lawful and filthy as pure.

Besides these, he encourages people to question the existence of the Almighty, and to debate His commandments. He forms doubts in people's minds regarding issues they do not understand. He persuades people to doubt the truth of matters regarding the faith and principles of Islam, and then he wants people to express these thoughts everywhere. We need to be aware that all of these tricks belong to Satan and take the necessary precautions. Our Lord informs us of these facts and instructs us to be on our toes:

O humankind! (Observe whatever God commands you. He has made you dwell on the earth, so) eat of what is on the earth provided it is lawful, and pure and wholesome (in composition and religiously); and do not follow in the footsteps of Satan (who deceives both those who are followed and those who follow); indeed he is a manifest enemy to you. He only commands you to evil and indecency and that you should speak against God the things about which you have no (sure) knowledge." (Baqara 2:168–169)

Treachery

The word *nifaq* (hypocrisy) is mainly used for being careless or indifferent toward religion. Treachery and hypocrisy combine to mean going back on your word and opposing righteousness in a devious manner.[4] Disloyalty to one's trust, going back on one's word and misusing trust are forms of betrayal. Treachery, or betrayal, is one of Satan's most palpable attributes.

Satan whispers the lowest and filthiest of acts into the minds of human beings. He decorates evil, giving it an innocent appearance. When he achieves his goal, he quickly leaves the scene of the crime. This is exactly how he approached Adam and his spouse. He appeared to be a sincere adviser, assuring them with all sorts of false promises. When they reached out to the forbidden tree, Satan disappeared from the scene. Hence, he left them all alone to face the consequences of their actions. The verse, *"Satan is but a traitor to man!"* (Furqan 25:29) points to this significant fact. Satan would never work for the good of man. Although sometimes he may appear to be a friend, his true objective is to ensure the downfall of man. Once man has fallen and is in need, Satan disappears. He will never abstain from treachery.

Satan is a depraved being; thus, he wishes to see humanity in a similar condition. He pushes human beings into loneliness, helplessness, disgrace, and despair.[5] He leads some human beings and jinn so astray that they become his followers and supporters. But Satan is disloyal and unfaithful, and when the time comes, he will deny everything, stating that he is unable to help any of his followers on the Day of Judgment:

> And Satan will say when the matter is decided, "Surely God promised you something that was bound to come true; I too promised but I failed you. And I had no power over you, except that I appealed to you, and you answered me. So do not blame

me, but blame yourselves. I cannot respond to your cry for help, nor can you respond to my cry for help. I reject your associating me as a partner with God (in belief or worship) in the past." Surely for the wrongdoers (who have wronged and ruined themselves by denying God or associating partners with Him) there is a painful punishment. (Ibrahim 14:22)

The foremost hypocrites and all those who follow them are coached by Satan. Although there is a difference between the words 'traitor' and 'hypocrite,' in essence they are used for the same purpose. Human beings learn two-facedness from Satan:

> (The hypocrites have deceived them) just like Satan, when he says to a human, "Disbelieve (in God)!" Then, when he disbelieves, he says (to the human), "Surely I am quit of you, for surely I fear God, the Lord of the worlds!" So the end of both (Satan and those whom he has deceived, and the hypocrites and those whom they have betrayed) is that they will find themselves in the Fire to abide therein. That is the recompense of the wrongdoers. (Hashr 59:16–17)

The only way to avoid Satan and his deceptions and to evade downfall in both this world and in the one after is to follow the ever straight path of God. Abdullah ibn Masud explains, "God's Messenger drew a straight line on the ground and said, 'This is the straight path of God.' Then, he drew various lines around it and stated, 'There are many other paths and on each of them there is Satan inviting you to join him.' Later, God's Messenger continued, *'This is my straight path, so follow it, and do not follow other paths, lest they scatter you from His path. This He has enjoined upon you, that you keep from disobedience to Him in reverence for Him and piety to deserve His protection,'*[6] reciting this verse."[7]

Whispers

The Arabic word *waswasa*, or 'Satan's whisper' carries different meanings such as 'a secret sound, sound of jewelry, speaking from within, or salacious thoughts.'[8] The word *waswass*, 'the whisperer,' is defined as 'a being who has an intense ability to hurl evil, useless, salacious, sleazy and deceitful thoughts into the hearts of human beings.' Due to his great ability in performing this, Satan is known as the whisperer. Secret whispers are his trait. The word *khunus* means 'contracted and concealed.'[9] It is also defined as 'constriction, withdrawal, gloominess, ominous, obscurity and to retreat.' On the other hand, subjective explanation of the word *khannas* is 'hiding or constraining upon hearing the name of God.'[10] We can summarize the meaning of the words *waswas* and *khannas* as 'the evil one, who pitches useless, indecent and unpleasant thoughts into the minds of human beings.' It is Satan who retreats and produces new strategies, and then deviously approaches again with his evil whispers to turn humankind away from their Lord.

"Satan sits on one's heart (waiting for the opportunity). If we remember God and recite His names, Satan constricts and surrenders to our will. However, if someone surrenders to heedlessness, then Satan begins to whisper into his heart."[11] In order to drag humans into heedlessness Satan embellishes worldly desires, driving humans into arrogance and vanity:

> Satan decked out their deeds to be appealing to them and said, "Today no power among humankind can overcome you, and for sure I am your supporter." But when the two hosts came within sight of each other, he turned on his heels to run away and said, "Indeed I am quit of you; surely I see that which you do not see. Indeed, I fear God." And God is severe in retribution. (Anfal 8:48)

This verse was revealed in relation to the Battle of Badr. Initially, Satan decorated the unbelievers' ideas and filled their hearts with arrogance. Upon witnessing the developments, he fled from the scene. Even as he was leaving, he argued, *"I am quit of you. I see that which you do not see. I fear God."* With his whispers he removed all hope from their hearts, leaving them alone with their painful fears.

In the Qur'an, the evidence regarding the whispers of Satan is described in the verses explaining the incident of Adam and Eve.[12]

Satan whispered into the hearts of Adam and Eve after being expelled from Paradise with the command *"Come out of there as an expellee!"* He sent whispers into the hearts of those who were still in Paradise. There are different explanations of this incident. Some have argued that Satan was prohibited from entering Paradise as honored angels do, but he was not banned from entering as a tool of test. Some claim that he came to the gates of Paradise and whispered from there. Others suggest that he took the shape of an animal so that the angels who guard the gates could not recognize him. There are claims that he entered by hiding in the mouth of a snake. There are also suggestions that he sent some of his aids to trick Adam and his spouse.[13] Only God knows the truth. The important thing here is that he was able to whisper into their hearts, even though he had been expelled from Paradise. When we analyze the verse, we realize that his expulsion did not prevent him attacking from all directions.

The noble Messenger described whispers as thoughts working to prevent a believer from performing his struggle, "Satan sits on the path of humanity. First, he says, 'Are you going to convert to Islam and leave the religion of your parents?' If he does not succeed, he then sits on the path of migration, and says, 'Where are you going? Are you leaving this beautiful land of yours?' If he fails again, then he sits on the path of war and argues, 'Battle consists of killing or dying. As a result your wealth will be distributed among others, and your wife will be someone else's spouse.' If the believer does not listen to this as well and continues his struggle on the path of God, then he shall enter paradise."[14]

Satan also attempted to whisper into the hearts of the Prophet's Companions in order to deceive them. Mikdad explains that on one occasion Satan whispered into his heart suggesting that he should drink the milk which was reserved for the noble Messenger. He was influenced by the whispers and drank the milk. He says that he regretted it later.[15] Satan also approached Abu Hurayra many times. Abu Hurayra suggested the recitation of *Ayat al-Kursiyy* (The Verse of the Throne)[16] for protection from Satan.[17]

There is no human being without a satan, but the distinction lies in obeying or opposing him. Aisha asked the noble Messenger, "Is Satan with me?" "He is with every human being," he replied. Then, Aisha asked, "Do you also have one?" The noble Prophet answered, "Yes, but with the help of God, mine has surrendered to me." In another hadith, God's Messenger said, "No human being is without a satan as companion." Upon this, his Companions asked, "Do you also have one?" He replied, "Yes, but with the help of God, he has surrendered to me. He only commands good deeds (now)."[18]

With the help of verses from the Qur'an and some hadiths, we have gathered some knowledge regarding the whispers of Satan. However, we can never acquire total understanding of his essence. For example, in the verse above, we do not know how he stated, *"Today no power among humankind can overcome you, and for sure I am your supporter."* How did he blame them and then flee? These are not the only mysteries. In many other verses there are terms such as his 'oath', 'companionship' and other interactions with humans. What is the fundamental nature of these occurrences? We may never have complete understanding of them because everything related to Satan occurs outside the boundaries of our dimensions. Just like his being, his acts are also occurrences of the metaphysical world. We know of him and his actions through the illumination of holy verses and hadiths, and hence we have total faith in the Qur'an and hadith."[19]

Besides all of this, one should also acknowledge the possibility that Satan's influence on humankind may be represented through a field of attraction or an atmosphere. The fact is that even those with righteous thoughts may experience a change of heart in an instant and begin to lean toward committing a sin. We could say that these individuals have been beguiled by his atmosphere, just like a piece of iron entering into the field of a magnet. Satan draws humankind into his field of attraction either by displaying a sin or by clouding a person's mind. Once we enter his field, Satan uses all of his capabilities to enslave us. Seeking refuge in God is a form of desire to defend oneself from falling into Satan's field.

Satan will never tire of whispering bad thoughts into the hearts and minds of human beings. If we allow even the tiniest opening or if we let our guard down even for an instant, he will attack. Evil thoughts and salacious memories generated either by Satan or a human's own carnal soul attack the heart of every human. In order to achieve victory, one must not fixate on these thoughts. Just like bees, they will increase their attacks if provoked. However, if one displays reluctance, they will diminish. If one observes the sun and the stars through a dirty pipe, the filth in the pipe will not affect the observed or the observer. In the same way, whispers and bad thoughts cannot harm the Divine Truth or the heart.[20]

According to Fethullah Gülen's summary of the topic of evil whispers, Satan and the carnal soul use evil whispers and bad thoughts to stop the human soul from augmentation on the path of Divine Truth. They disgrace human beings by manipulating their intelligence, crippling their free will and breaking their enthusiasm. They try to accomplish this by pushing them into transitory pleasures and caprice.

The heart is the primary center of reflection for satanic whispers. From there they spread to the other organs. This is why their initial effects are felt by the heart. When the mind is preoccupied with these thoughts, the heart also begins to feel their effect. This is exactly what Satan wishes to achieve; he has come a step closer to his aim. Nevertheless, a whisper rejected by the heart has no detrimental effect. The reason for this is that the whisper has no further effect than being a part of the imagination. Imagination is not a physical act, and therefore it cannot be considered a bad deed. Feeling distressed about the whole issue is an indication that the heart has rejected the whisper.

The intensity of the heart's rejection is proportional to one's degree of faith. Yes, the heart will retaliate depending on the strength of one's faith. Sometimes, one assumes that the reaction shown by the heart is a sign of approval. Those who fall into this situation feel severe anxiety and stress. Some people feel the need to escape from this situation by fleeing from the Divine Presence to enter a phase of somnolence. However, there is no evidence suggesting an approval by the heart. It is a mere reaction. In fact this reaction manifests the strength and firmness of one's faith. This is why the Messenger of God makes the following statement, "This is faith itself,"[21] when referring to this condition for complete clarification.[22]

Being cursed and damned

Satan has many traits, all of which he uses to achieve his goals. He replaced all good qualities—which he willfully eliminated—with evil ones and then constantly enhanced his iniquitous attributes. This resembles a person who uses his free will only in the name of evil, gradually closing all doors to righteousness. He also possesses two negative attributes—being cursed and damned. These are the two signs stamped on his forehead for rebelling against Almighty God.

Satan had many abilities even prior to his rebellion. He possessed the potential for decorating, whispering and sedition even before the creation of Adam. However, he had never used nor did he have a reason to use them earlier. These characteristics of Satan were not manifested because they had not surfaced yet. When he was ordered to bow down before Adam, he was arrogant and refused stubbornly. At this point, he began to show his true colors. Two new attributes were added to the rest of his evil features. From that moment on, he was cursed and expelled from Paradise.

La'nat means 'to be cursed and expelled with condemnation.' It is defined as 'driven away, distanced from the Creator.' It also carries the meanings of 'being dishonored and cursed by the Creator.' This word also indicates punishment because one who is kept away from God would enter hell for eternity. The word *la'nat* is the most evident attribute of Satan, since he was expelled from the heavens and driven away from God's mercy. The word *lain* also has the meaning of 'being cursed and disgraced.'[23] Asım Efendi concludes that the word 'cursed' means 'to be driven away. It refers to a being which is hated, damned, dishonored, and desecrated by everyone.[24]

In the Qur'an Satan is mentioned along with polytheism and the verse describes how he was cursed by God:

> Indeed God does not forgive that partners be associated with Him; less than that He forgives to whomever He wills (whomever He has guided to repentance and righteousness as a result of his choosing repentance and righteousness by his free will). Whoever associates partners with God has indeed strayed far away (from the Straight Path). In His stead, they invoke female deities—(in so doing) they in fact invoke none but a haughty, rebellious Satan, one who is accursed by God (excluded from His mercy). Once he said, "Of Your servants I will surely take a share to be assigned to me (by their following me). I will surely lead them astray and surely engross them in vain desires (superstitious fancies and false conceptions); and I will surely command them, and they will surely slit the ears of cattle (to mark them out as meant for their idols and as forbidden to themselves to eat, thus making a lawful thing unlawful); and also I will surely command them and they will surely alter God's creation." Whoever takes Satan for a confidant and guardian instead of God has indeed suffered a manifest loss. (In reality, however, Satan has no authority over people against God.) He makes promises to them and fills them with vain desires (superstitious fancies and false conceptions), and what he promises them is nothing but delusion. (Nisa 4:116–120)

It is quite obvious in this verse why Satan was cursed. Not only did he refuse to obey God's command, but he also insolently attempted to justify his rebellion: *"He said, Do You see this that You have honored above me? Indeed, if You grant me respite till the Day of Resurrection, I will certainly bring his descendants under my sway, all but a few!"'* (Isra 17:62) He also brought God's wrath upon himself by many other disrespectful acts:

> He (God) said, "Go your way! Whoever of them follows you—surely, Hell will be the recompense of you all, a recompense most ample! Arouse with your (seductive) voice whomever you can from among them, and rally against them with

your cavalry and foot soldiers, and be their partner in their
wealth and children, and make promises to them." And Satan
promises them nothing but deceit. (Isra 17:63–64)

The word *rajim*—also an attribute of Satan—has many interpretations such as 'to cast stones, to kill, to curse, to be separated,
to drive out, to falsely suspect, to use foul language and to calum-
niate.' Literally, it means 'to be expelled, dishonored, cursed or
stoned.' The word *rajim* applies to both the perpetrator and the
recipient. Satan is *rajim* so besides being a curser, seducer, instigator, whisperer, calumniator and an insulter, he is also the cursed,
stoned, expelled, driven out, disgraced, and dishonored. There is a
slight difference in the words *lain* (cursed) and *rajim* (rejected).
These terms have the quality of interconnection which suggests
that they may be inserted within each other. *Lain* is 'the one whose
ties with good have been disconnected and broken.' *Rajim*, on the
other hand, is 'being expelled with dishonor and disgrace.' One
who has been driven away from the presence of God has also been
denounced and disgraced. Therefore, everything which represents
good has eternally been closed for him. Yes, one who brings the
wrath of God upon himself shall be cursed. Rebellion to God is
punishable by condemnation and banishment. Consequently, one
who falls into this situation will be rejected and affronted by all.

The Qur'an informs us that the heavens have been ornamented
by God and protected from all the satans of *rajim*: *"We have assuredly set in the heaven great constellations, and We have made it (the
heaven) beautiful for those beholding; and We have made it secure
against every accursed Satan rejected (from God's mercy)"* (Hijr 15:16–
17). The phrase *"every accursed Satan rejected"* indicates that all
satans, whether in the form of humans or jinn, are regarded as
rajim, accursed and rejected. Satan and his followers cannot ascend
to the heavens to continue their quest for malevolence as they do
on earth. They have no authority there. The heavens are shut to all
satans. They have all been expelled from the heavens. Although
they long to steal information from the heavens to use on earth,

they face a blazing fire which constantly pursues them. Almighty God informs us that the heavens are protected from all types of satans.

Just like the heavens, the holy Qur'an is also protected by God. Hence, no one has the power to do any harm to it: *"Indeed it is We, We Who send down the Reminder in parts, and it is indeed We Who are its Guardian"* (Hijr 15:9). There are three similarities between the holy Qur'an and the heavens. First, there is the similarity of the Qur'an and the heavens. Just as the grandeur and beauty of the heavens is spellbinding, we are also mesmerized by the unique manner and the inimitable verses of the holy Qur'an. Second, there is the similarity of the verses mentioning the protection of the Qur'an and the heavens; God has placed both the Qur'an and the heavens under his protection. Third, when the protection of the heavens is mentioned, the holy Qur'an refers to satans as *rajim*; similarly, before we begin to recite the holy Qur'an, we are ordered to seek refuge in God from the satans: *"When you recite the Qur'an, seek refuge in God from Satan eternally rejected from God's mercy"* (Nahl 16:98).

Ordering evil and wickedness

All beauty and good is from God, and He does not like ungratefulness in His servants:[25]

> God enjoins justice (and right judgment in all matters), and devotion to doing good, and generosity toward relatives, and He forbids you indecency, wickedness and vile conduct (all offenses against religion, life, personal property, chastity, and health of mind and body). He exhorts you (repeatedly) so that you may reflect and be mindful! (Nahl 16:90)

Worship performed with comprehension prevents human beings from committing bad deeds. The Qur'an offers the daily prayers as an example, *"and establish the Prayer in conformity with its conditions. Surely, the Prayer restrains from all that is indecent and shameful, and all that is evil*" (Ankabut 29:45). The only thing humankind should pursue is the pleasing of God and His noble Messenger.

All-Merciful God commands human beings to take the middle path, the straight path. He forbids extremism and indolence and commands that we worship only Him. He said to the noble Messenger, "*Adopt the way of forbearance and tolerance, and enjoin what is good and right, and withdraw from the ignorant ones*" (A'raf 8:199). It is one of God's principles to command righteousness and virtue. Just like his Lord, the noble Messenger also commands the performance of good and forbids the doing of evil. When the holy Qur'an talks about believers, it associates them with the same qualities of ordering good and forbidding evil.[26]

Satan, on the other hand, commands exactly the opposite:

> Never let Satan seduce you (and cause you to fail in similar trials) as he caused your (ancestral) parents to be driven out of the Garden, pulling off from them their garment and revealing to them their private parts (and the carnal impulses ingrained in them). He sees you and his host (see you) from where you do not see them. We have made satans the confidants and fellow-criminals of those who do not believe. And whenever they commit an indecency, they say (attempting to excuse themselves), "We found our parents doing that (and follow in their footsteps), and this is what God has enjoined on us." Say, "Indeed, God does not enjoin indecency. Or is it that you speak about God things you have no knowledge of?" (A'raf 7:27–28)

We must not forget that for those who rebel against God and His Messenger, there is a fire in which they shall dwell for eternity as disgraced and dishonored beings.

Rebellion and stubbornness

For Satan, his rebellion is the beginning of the end. Thus, his obstinacy has established his inevitable fate. He rejected the divine command and refused to bow down before Adam. His rebellion of "opposing the command of the Lord"[27] was the first wrong he com-

mitted. When he was ordered, he became arrogant and disrespect-
fully refused. The Qur'an says, *"(God) said, 'What prevented you from
prostrating when I commanded you to do so?' Iblis said, 'I am better than
he, for You have created me from fire, and him You have created from
clay'"* (A'raf 7:12). Satan showed no remorse for refusing to bow,
which made him disrespectful in his reply. Hence, this was his second great error. He had rebelled and persisted obstinately.
Nevertheless, he had the chance to save himself, if only he had
shown remorse, instead of stubbornness. For Adam realized his
mistake and pleaded for forgiveness, and so it was granted. Satan
failed to do this, and there was no sign of goodwill to make up for
his mistake. This is why his rebellion became a part of his personali-
ty and distinguished him from others. Where revolt against the
Almighty is concerned, we think of rebellion, and when we think of
rebellion, it reminds us of Satan. When Abraham said to his father,
*"O my father! Do not worship Satan (by obeying his suggestions to you to
worship idols)! Satan is ever rebellious against the All-Merciful,"*[28] he
was referring to this particular characteristic of Satan.

Obedience is the opposite of rebellion. Therefore, obeying
God is considered the same as rebelling against Satan and vice
versa. So, those who perform their prayers will not be influenced
by Satan's deception and—by the will of God—they will refrain
from wrongful acts. This also means to befriend God. Satan said,
*"If You will but respite me to the Day of Judgment, I will surely bring
his descendants under my sway—all but a few!"* With the words *"all
but a few"* he was referring to the righteous servants of God. Satan
knows that no matter which diabolical strategy he uses and no
matter from which direction he approaches, he will fail to manipulate those who perform their prayers in sincerity. God defends his
sincere servants with the following verse: *"But as for My (sincere,
devoted) servants—you will have no authority over them"* (Isra 17:65).

Choosing Satan as a companion means turning away from God:
*"Whoever takes Satan for a confidant and guardian instead of God has
indeed suffered a manifest loss"* (Nisa 4:119). Rebelling against God

and befriending Satan is an attribute of an unbeliever. Following the path of the rebellious Satan means rebellion against God. A friend of the enemy is also considered an enemy. Our interaction with Satan is proportional to our degree of faith. Those without faith chose satans as their companions, friends or bosses: *"We have made satans the confidants and fellow-criminals of those who do not believe"* (A'raf 7:27). There is an attraction between infidelity and Satan. An unprotected garden will be infested with pests: *"Do you not see that We send the satans upon the unbelievers (because of their unbelief), and they impel them (toward sin and every kind of evil) with strong impulsion?"* (Maryam 19:83). As this verse suggests, Satan infests the hearts of unbelievers. Unbelievers enjoy satanic activities, and they are obsessed with Satan's features. Useless people will only make friends with contagious people like themselves. Unbelievers have a propensity toward satanic behavior. Hence, Satan becomes their leader, dragging them to wherever he wishes.[29]

Exploitation of fear

Fear is a powerful emotion. It is a psychological phase which occurs in the event of an assumption or supposition that one is in danger of being harmed. The emotion of hope is quite similar, but it is a period of waiting for something pleasant to occur. Security is the opposite of fear, and it is used both in our worldly affairs and in religious terminology. The phrase 'fear of God' does not mean to be afraid as one would be of a ferocious lion or tiger, nor does it mean one should keep away from Him. The best analogy for this fear would be the fear that a child feels toward his parents. When a child makes a mistake, he knows that his parents will be upset and he feels afraid, but this feeling does not prevent him from continuing to love his parents. Just as in this example, human beings love and fear God at the same time. A believer is aware of His infinite mercy and eternal punishment. Like a child that runs back to her mother's arms after being punished, when God-fearing people commit a sin, instead of distancing themselves, they turn back to God. They wish to be judged, while seeking refuge in His mercy. As described by the hadith, the one who has sinned takes refuge in God from God.

From this perspective, fear of God means to restrain oneself from forbidden activities and to become profound with worship. So, this suggests that one who persists in committing sins has no fear of God. Therefore, abstaining from activities which lead to rebellion and encouraging others to do the same is a sign of fearing God: *"For them will be dark layers of the Fire above them, and dark layers below them. With this does God warn off His servants. O My servants, keep from disobedience to Me in reverence for Me and piety and so deserve My protection."* (Zumar 39:16). God forbids believers from fearing Satan and his aids, *"It was but the devil who (by provoking alarm) desires to make you fearful of his allies. So do not fear them but fear Me, if you are (true) believers"* (Imran 3:175). We can interpret this verse as "Do not obey Satan's commands, but obey and submit only to My commands." The first part of the verse above may be interpreted as "Satan threatens you with his aids" or "You are being threatened by Satan's aids."

Satan generates fear in the human heart, or he forms fear in the hearts of his aids. He may also manipulate some of his aids to form fear in the hearts of others. In order to lead human beings astray, Satan wishes to use the emotion of fear to his advantage. Believers should engage in activities which restrict Satan's space for operation. They should channel their sentiment of fear toward respecting God and obeying His commandments and refraining from sins.

False promises and pledges

The Arabic word *wa'd*, or 'pledge,' can be interpreted as 'a promise, a given word, assurance or a guarantee.' It can be used both in a positive manner and a negative one. Satan promises his followers unrealistic things which he can never deliver. He works on their imaginations and desires by giving them mouth-watering expectations and prospects. The promises he makes follow the path of evil, and they are nothing but deceptions: "*Satan makes promises to them, and fills them with vain desires, and what he promises them is nothing but delusion*" (Nisa 4:120). Satan directs people to various expectations and assumptions. Since he continuously works for the demise of man, he spreads despondency about virtue and good deeds: "*Satan frightens you with poverty and bids you into indecencies*" (Baqara 2:268). He attacks with conjectures and thoughts like "Do not give to charity. Do not be an altruist, for you will lose everything you have. You will be poor."

On the other hand, he adorns wrongful acts, presenting them in attractive packages. He distributes nothing but deceptive desires. Those who get swept away by these false hopes cannot foresee what lies ahead. This is why those subjected to these kind of attacks usually surrender, falling into unrealistic expectations and false anticipations. Thus, they fail to discover the truth and grace.

Satan's false promises and pledges apply to everyone. No one is exempt from his attacks. Satan whispers suspicion and doubt. He throws ideas into people's minds, ornamenting them to look appealing. Sometimes these desires may not be effective, but mistakes are probable for everyone. Even Prophets were not excluded. The only thing that distinguishes Prophets is that God protects them from Satan's mischief, and therefore they are not harmed:

> Never did We send a Messenger or a Prophet before you but that when he recited (God's Revelations to the people) Satan would make insinuations (about these Revelations, prompting people to misconstrue them in many wrong senses, rather than the right one). But God abrogates whatever insinuations Satan may make, and then He confirms and establishes His Revelations. God is All-Knowing, All-Wise. (Hajj 22:52)

In the case of Prophets, if a decision belongs to them, that is, if they are not directed by Divine revelation, then on a rare occasion they may also lapse. However, God immediately removes these thoughts thrown in by Satan. Then, He replaces them with His Signs allowing no room for doubts. If Satan was permitted to influence Prophets, there would be no difference between a Prophet's aspiration and a hypocrite's heart of stone. God disabled Satan's ability to deceive Prophets; therefore, Prophets were not left alone with their thoughts and desires. God protected the Divine Revelations received by the Prophets. This way, they were assured that God was the source of their inspiration and that it was the whole truth. This in turn enabled them to perform their mission without any doubts or hesitation.

However, in order to be tested, everyone else is left alone with their thoughts and desires. Whilst those with pure and benign hearts succeed, others with ailing hearts fail. Almighty God explains,

> He makes Satan's insinuations a trial for those in the center of whose hearts is a sickness and who have hardened hearts (that extinguishes their power of understanding and corrupts their character). The wrongdoers have certainly veered far from the truth and are in wide schism. (Hajj 22:53)

The reason for this is that they have wasted their lives on chasing the desires of their carnal selves, and whilst they were given the chance to find the truth, they insisted on iniquity. Their stoneheartedness comes from their rebuttal of repentance and their refusal to turn toward God.

Human beings are filtered by many different trials in life. Those who face difficult situations should seek refuge in God and plead for His help. Seeking refuge in God is the manifestation of the interaction which exists between humans and their Lord. Unless human beings behave in this manner, their hearts will harden and become more and more distant from God. Hardening of the heart also speeds up the process of becoming tangled in Satan's web. This means that being heedless and disrespectful of God hardens the heart; this in turn allows one to be deceived by Satan. God says in the Qur'an, "*If only, when Our trial came upon them, they had invoked Us with humility! But their hearts grew hard and Satan decked out whatever they were doing as appealing to them*" (An'am 6:43). Worshipping God will prevent the hardening of the heart and will form a barrier against Satan's assaults. The verse describes those who turn away from God and become stone-hearted; this makes them vulnerable to Satan's false promises and assurances.

Measuring every thought and idea by the teachings of the Qur'an and hadith and organizing one's life according to them is the sign of a righteous heart. God knows best; perhaps this is the secret to achieving victory through all types of test.

Deception by decoration

The holy Qur'an describes Satan's ability to decorate with the words *tazyin* and *taswil*. According to the dictionary, *tazyin* is 'announcing the beauty of something with words or behavior.'[30] It also carries the meanings 'to decorate, to approbate, to entice, to make it easier and to deceive.' Sometimes, God uses the verb 'decorating' in relation to Himself, sometimes in association with Satan and sometimes He assigns it to an unknown agent.[31] The word *taswil*, on the other hand, is defined as 'the decoration of lust desired by the carnal soul or displaying the ugly sides of mania as if they were attractive.' The holy Qur'an attributes this trait to Satan and the carnal soul.

When the Qur'an mentions worldly things that human beings enjoy and desire, *tazyin* is used in an indefinite form: *"Made innately appealing to men are passionate love for women, children, (hoarded) treasures of gold and silver, branded horses, cattle, and plantations. Such are enjoyments of the present, worldly life; yet with God is the best of the goals to pursue"* (Imran 3:14). The worldly desires mentioned here are decorated and presented as appealing before human beings, and they become fond of them with the assumption that these are the things that are meant to be loved. There is a legitimate side to all of these desires, but they may also be obtained by illegitimate means. The first option refers to a decoration by God. The second option, however, refers to decorations by Satan and by the ignorance of human beings. This is why they are criticized at the end of the verse.[32]

Almighty God is the Creator of everything, yet He assigns the attributes of *tazyin* and *taswil* to Satan, and He brings Satan's abilities to manipulate to our attention:

> Satan decked out their deeds to be appealing to them and said, "Today no power among humankind can overcome you, and for sure I am your supporter." But when the two hosts came within sight of each other, he turned on his heels to run away and said, "Indeed I am quit of you; surely I see that which you do not see. Indeed, I fear God." And God is severe in retribution. (Anfal 8:48)

Satan convinced the polytheists of Mecca that they would taste victory over the Muslims in the event of a war, simply because they possessed more weaponry and they were greater in numbers. The idea of victory was so adroitly decorated in their minds that, according to their egos, they were invincible. Satan would also join them and never leave their side. However, this was not to be. As soon as the two armies met and things began to turn in favor of the Muslims, Satan did exactly what his nature suggested and fled. Not only did he leave them on their own, but he also blamed them for all the evil acts. Following his discouraging remarks, he abandoned them to their despair, transforming their sweetest dreams into nightmares. Then, he left the scene to speed up the process of their inevitable fate.

Those who have fallen into Satan's decorated deceptions are like those who wander away from the straight path and fall into the abyss of atheism and hypocrisy, in awareness of the fact that the truth of God's religion has been clearly manifested to them: *"Surely those who have turned back as apostates after (God's) guidance has become clear to them, Satan has seduced them; he has implanted in them long-term worldly ambitions."* (Muhammad 47:25) They are exposed to Satan's deception. There were those who denied the Qur'an instead of taking God's Word as guidance. They argued, "We shall accept some of its commandments." Little did they know that they were betraying the Qur'an. This was an act of treason which drew the wrath of God upon them. They had no intention to please God. So, God completely overturned the plans of these hypocrites.

Ignoring the Qur'an, disregarding its magnificent perfection, joining the ranks of those who rebel against God, and deviating from the straight path are all acts of being misled by Satan and his traits of *tazyin* and *taswil*. What we can gather from this is that Satan's deceptions and instigations do not rain upon us without a cause. When one insists on rejecting what is good and holy, the gates are left ajar, and Satan's invitation is sent.

Satan's deception, whispers, trickery, and diabolical plots can only be effective when human beings display weakness. The only prevention is to lead a pious life without leaving any gaps for Satan's attacks. Satan himself admits this reality:

> Iblis said, "My Lord! Because You have allowed me to rebel and go astray, I will indeed deck out to be appealing to them on the earth (the worldly , material dimension of human existence and the path of error), and I will surely cause them all to rebel and go astray, except Your servants from among them, endowed with sincerity in faith and Your worship." (Hijr 15:39–40)

The last phrase (*except your servants...*) reveals Satan's weakness. In his description, he gives the characteristics of those who cannot be deceived. Indeed, Satan will not find the opportunity to attack those who have no free time for worldly pleasures and decorated desires.

Another aspect of Satan's character is that he presents falsehood as truth causing confusion in weak minds. This is called *talbis*, which means 'to cause a matter to assume the appearance of something different.' Satan attempts to persuade people to accept superstition as truth or reality. Besides using their ignorance and lack of knowledge, he also makes use of intelligence and knowledge to mislead people into wrong directions. He waits obstinately for the right opportunity, and as soon as he sees an opening, he attacks. The great scholar Hasan Basri was asked, "Does Satan sleep?" He replied, "If he did then we would have a breather."[33] How fitting is the proverb, "Water sleeps but Satan does not."

Instigation and mischief

Satan uses instigation to incite the emotions of conflict, so that he may cause discord among human beings. He provokes with words of anger and antagonism. Using a strategy of intrigue, he wishes to bring humans to their knees. This strategy could be described as provocation ŏr sedition, and it is done to agitate people into involvement in certain matters by manipulating their feelings of retaliation. At the instigation of Satan, one enters into a phase of trepidation and looks for ways to strike back.

Satan was the instigator behind the incident which occurred between Joseph and his brothers. Joseph's father, Jacob, warned him, "*Oh my son! Do not relate your dream to your brothers, lest they devise a scheme against you. For Satan is a manifest enemy to humankind (and can incite them to do such a thing)*" (Yusuf 12:5). Almighty God also warns us of Satan's instigations, "*And say to My servants that they should always speak (even when disputing with others) that which is the best. Satan is ever ready to sow discord among them. For Satan is a manifest enemy for humankind*" (Isra 17:53). So, Satan's instigations can come at any time, and on most occasions, human beings fall into his trap. The best way for people to protect themselves is to seek refuge in God: "*If a prompting from Satan should stir in you (when carrying out your mission or during worship or in your daily life), seek refuge in God immediately*" (Fussilat 41:36). For, we can only be protected from all forms of evil by taking asylum in our Lord.

In almost every verse which mentions Satan's instigation and deception, the holy Qur'an talks about being well-mannered and speaking words of virtue. It mentions the virtues of being compassionate and merciful. The Qur'an uses this method because this is the only way Satan's deception can be avoided or opposed.

Causing forgetfulness

The Arabic word *nisyan* can be defined as 'to fail to remember, to overlook, fail to recall, disregard or to put out of one's mind.' It is the exact opposite of memorizing. Those who know themselves will also know God. Hence, those who forget themselves will fail to remember God. This is why God commands, *"And remember and mention Him (straightaway) should you forget"* (Kahf 18:24). The second meaning of *nisyan* is 'to abandon or renounce,' and this occurs due to weakening of the heart, or indolence, or it can be intentional: "So, *taste the punishment because you acted in oblivious heedlessness of this Day"* (Sajda 32:14). Then, we are also warned in the following verse: *"when He bestows a favour upon him, he forgets for what he prayed to Him before"* (Zumar 39:8). These verses refer to issues related to God, and when they are forgotten or intentionally renounced, human beings will be held accountable.

There are also situations where certain things are unintentionally forgotten. In relation to this, the noble Prophet states, "Responsibility has been lifted from my people for things they are forced to do, issues they forget and for unintentional errors they make."[34] Perhaps the noble Prophet is clarifying the different meanings of forgetting.

In some verses of the Qur'an, the word forgetting is associated with God. However, God does not forget. It is used in a different sense, such as, 'God punishes or condemns.' The following verse is an example, *"you acted in oblivious heedlessness of this Day. We are now oblivious and heedless of you"* (Sajda 32:14). Indeed, they will not be forgotten by God, but they will be treated as if they have been forgotten.

When we tackle the issue of forgetfulness from two different angles, we realize that there is liability in one case, but a valid excuse is acceptable in the other. For example, a person detects dirt on his clothes but does not attend to it immediately. Later he performs his prayer, failing to remember that he had to clean his garment first. In this case, there is no valid excuse because he should have cleaned it at first sight. However, his excuse would have been acceptable if he had performed his prayer unaware of the dirt on his clothes. By this token, we can say that if a person displays reluctance toward learning the principles of religion or fails to remember what he has learnt because of lack of practice or review, then his excuse of forgetfulness is not valid.[35]

It is in man's nature to forget and everyone is forgetful to a certain degree. Even Prophets are not excluded from this. God warns His Messenger against forgetfulness, commanding him to stay away from polytheists. If, however, the Prophet forgets and sits with them, God instructs him to walk away as soon as he recalls:

> When you meet such as indulge in (blasphemous or derisive) talk about Our Revelations, turn away from them until they engage in some other talk. And should Satan cause you to forget, no longer remain, after recollection, in the company of such wrongdoing people. (An'am 6:68)

In this verse, forgetfulness is associated with Satan, but it also suggests that it is possible even for a Prophet to forget.

Prophet Moses decided to visit Al-Khidr, taking along a young man. When they stopped on the way, Moses asked the youth to take out the fish they had brought along to eat. When the young man tried to explain how he had left the fish behind, he said, *"Would you believe it? When we betook ourselves to that rock for a rest, I forgot about (our cooked) fish—and none but Satan caused me to forget to mention it (to you)"* (Kahf 18:63). He associated the incident of forgetting with Satan.

The noble Prophet also confirms that Satan is the cause of forgetfulness. Abu Hurayra explains, "One day God's Messenger came to the Masjid and walked over to his usual place of prayer. There were two lines consisting of men and a line of women waiting for him. He then turned toward them and said, 'If Satan causes me to forget something from my prayer, men should say *tasbih* (reciting *subhanallah*) and women should clap their hands.' The noble Messenger then led the prayer and did not forget anything from his prayer."[36]

When the Qur'an mentions the status of hypocrites, it states, *"Satan has subdued them and so caused them to forget remembrance of God. Those are the party of Satan. Be aware: the party of Satan, they are the losers (the self-ruined)"* (Mujadila 58:19). As a matter of fact, hypocrites have not really forgotten God; they are only pretending not to remember. They are unenthusiastic about God and His religion. Because of their circumventing the remembrance of God for a very long time, their good qualities have diminished, gradually transforming them into satans. They have entered into a vicious circle as Satan did before them. Satan was expelled from Paradise for refusing to obey God, and this in turn triggered the development of antagonism within him. He distanced himself so far from God that mercy had become unreachable for him. Hypocrites also follow the same path. They wander so far away from the truth that it causes them to join Satan's party. Consequently, they dig a hole so deep for themselves that escape becomes impossible.

Ignoring God is the beginning of a great disaster. Turning a blind eye to the remembrance of God and closing one's ears to the Qur'anic truth is an invitation to Satan's dominion. Hence, the Qur'an states:

> Whoever willfully ignores the remembrance of the All-Merciful (and lives as if He did not exist always watching him), We assign to him a devil, who becomes his closest comrade. Such devils certainly bar them from the way (of truth). Yet they think (in themselves) that they are rightly guided. But in the end, when such a one comes to Us (on Judgment Day), he says (to his comrade), "Ah, would that between me and you were the distance of the two easts. How evil a comrade!" (Zukhruf 43:36–38)

In conclusion, we can say that Satan causes forgetfulness and negligence. Besides causing people to forget some simple issues, he also hopes to see humanity in despair, both in this world and in the one after, by deleting important matters such as prayers, the holy Book, and supplication to God from their minds.

His touch

In religious terminology, 'being touched by Satan' indicates mental illness or insanity. The Arabic word *mamsus* (touched) is also used for those who suffer from epileptic seizures. Some believe that since the cause of these types of illnesses are unknown, they may be related to satanic possession. There has been a lot of controversy surrounding the issue of possession; however, the real interpretation is clear.

During the era of ignorance, usury was so common that it became part of social life. When Islam abolished usury, in order to illustrate its ugliness, usurers were likened to those who were possessed by Satan: *"As to those who consume interest (even though they seem for a time to be making a profit), they turn out like one whom Satan has bewitched and confounded by his touch (and they will rise up from their graves in the same way before God)"* (Baqara 2:275). Elmalılı Hamdi Yazır explains, "Since they have filled their guts with interest gained from usury, on the Day of Judgment they will be resurrected as madmen. This feature will separate them from the rest."[37]

When the severity of Prophet Job's illness became unbearable, he said, *"Satan has touched me with distress and suffering"* (Sa'd 38:41). He defined his situation as being touched by Satan. The scholar Qurtubi explains Satan's affliction of Prophet Job as "reaching Prophet Job through whispers of deception."[38] Elmalılı Hamdi Yazır describes Satan's touch as "finding means to whisper deception."[39] Moreover, Fakhraddin Razi interprets it as "Satan inviting to lust, sensuality, and other activities which keep man away from God. Hence, this is his touch."[40] Baydawi, however, relates Satan's touch to mental illness.[41]

What we can gather from all this is that Satan constantly looks for ways to take man into the valley of malevolence by using various systematic approaches. He wishes to destroy man's eternal happiness; thus, all these ways may be described as his touch.

METHODS OF APPROACH

Lust and sensuality

There are many tools which Satan uses to lead man astray. In order to achieve his evil goals, he will use methods that one cannot even imagine. Lust is one of the weaknesses of humankind. Lust can be defined as 'passionate desire, envy, and longing for a desired object' or, as suggested by some, 'giving your heart to your desires.' Abu Ubayd said, "Some people conceive lust as an emotion felt toward the opposite sex." Ibn Manzur states, "I think it is wrong to delineate lust by using a single definition. It consists of all sins which the perpetrator conceals. Sins which human beings commit in secret and do not wish for others to find out can be defined as hidden lust."[42] The noble Prophet defines sin in the same line, "Sin is a thing that exerts weight on your conscience, and it is something you do not wish others to know."[43] The hidden lust or desires described in this hadith may give some idea about the connection which exists between sin and lust.

God also did not define lust only as feelings toward the opposite sex: *Made innately appealing to men are passionate love for women, children, (hoarded) treasures of gold and silver, branded horses, cattle, and plantations. Such are enjoyments of the present, worldly life; yet with God is the best of the goals to pursue* (Imran 3:14).

Although lust should not be interpreted only as a desire toward the opposite sex, it is usually the first thing that comes to mind. In the verse above, when listing the things that attract man's attention the most, Almighty God mentions women first. The noble Prophet points to this fact by saying, "I will not leave behind a harder test for men than the one they will face with women."[44] Desire for women is the most powerful factor that drives men astray. Indeed, women are to men, what men are to women. Since the beginning of time, each sex has been tested with the other. Explaining that he was also equipped with the same emotions, the Prophet said that he was made to love women and pleasant fragrance in this world. Just like other men, he was also a human being. However, there was a distinctive quality about him which separated him from the rest of the human race. He received Revelation and the heavens were his friend. Besides this, God's Messenger smiled and wept, ate and drank, spoke and remained silent. He would frequently mix with people and participate in social activities.

The Prophet experienced most tests—inevitable for every human being—and taught others how to behave in such situations. One day, he caught a glimpse of a woman and then rushed to his wife Zaynab. At that moment, Zaynab was cleaning a piece of leather. After being with her, God's Messenger came to his Companions and said, "Sometimes, women arrive and leave in the form of Satan. If one feels like he is being tempted by a woman, then he should immediately go to his wife so this will satisfy his carnal self."[45] According to scholars, a female appearing as Satan is an analogy referring to seductive feelings which incite men into various desires. This is because God created man's carnal self with a proclivity toward women.[46]

We should make it clear that, women with bad intentions who divert men out of the right path are likened to Satan. However, in general women find their true position in Islam, receiving the respect and esteem they deserve. From this perspective, we realize that men who encourage women into immoral behavior also appear in the form of satans.

Uthman ibn Madh'un once came to the Prophet asking for permission to seclude himself to worship so that he might abstain from the pleasures of the flesh indefinitely. The Prophet rejected his request and advised him to fast. Sa'd ibn Muadh says, "If the Prophet had given him permission, we would have castrated ourselves in order to break our lust (so that we could endure the difficulties of being unmarried)."[47]

Satan commands adultery and encourages indecency. He makes this kind of life seem as attractive as possible. He promotes flirting. Yet, an explosion is inevitable when gunpowder is left next to fire. All of the above are outside the boundary drawn by Islam.

Lust is a potential which exists in every human being. However, controlling it or restricting it to a minimum is always possible. The solution is provided in the hadith mentioned above. One should either get married, fast, or control one's diet. The human stomach is the source of lust and various illnesses. When it is full, the attraction between women and men increases. If we control our carnal self with hunger, Satan's area of operation becomes restricted. One of the benefits of eating less is that it barricades the channel which lust uses to attack, and forms a shield against the invasion of the carnal self. Hunger narrows Satan's passageways as he travels through the human blood vessels. This is also a means of escaping from his domination to attain peace. As a matter of fact, peace and happiness depend on our control over our carnal desires.

Fame and hypocrisy

Prominence and passion for fame is one of Satan's favored tools of deception. Fame, a thing desired by people, has an ugly manifestation. This definition is supported by the following hadith: "Whoever wears the garment of fame, God makes them wear the garment of degradation." Hammad al-Jawhari, the renowned scholar of Arabic, defines fame as 'the revealing of an act.' This in turn is defined as a 'scandal.'[48]

Those on the journey toward eternity should work for the life after death, show effort by raising their standards and achieve depth in their worship. Otherwise, God's approval of their worship will not be enough for them, and so they will seek the acknowledgment of others. A person knows that he will be praised by others if he abstains from his desires and dedicates his life to worship. They will come to him for salvation, asking for his blessings and prayers. Consequently, he will choose the attention and affection of people over God's approval. He will continue to assume that he is close to God, not realizing that his name has been entered into the book of hypocrites. On this issue, Ghazali says, "This is one of the biggest webs Satan spins. Only those who truly believe can protect themselves from this. This passage is so deep and narrow that only those close to God may pass through. For this reason, it is said that the last thing a man of truth (*siddiq*) would want is the love of rank or high position."[49]

There is a fine line between fame and hypocrisy. They both occur when we attempt to gain a spot in the hearts of people by trying to impress. In religious terms, hypocrisy is attributed to those who wish to be praised for being a righteous and pious person. "Hypocrisy is the most dangerous thing, since it makes less noise than an ant's footsteps as it enters the heart. Besides those who possess no knowledge regarding the weaknesses of the heart, even scholars of great caliber are at risk."[50] In the matter of fame, desired recognition is sought in areas other than worship. Those who show reluctance in their prayers and perform them in a hurry are mentioned along with hypocrites in the Qur'an.[51]

Hypocrisy is also expectation and desires that blemish the purity of worship. The verse, *"Never did We send a Messenger or a Prophet before you but that when he recited (God's Revelations to the people) Satan would make insinuations (about these Revelations, prompting people to misconstrue them in many wrong senses, rather than the right one)"* (Hajj 22:52), clearly points to the fact that even Prophets are not excluded from Satan's attacks. "It does not befit a Prophet to frame aspirations as they cannot be purified of desires and imagination. Satan meddles with aspirations. Others aside, even when a Prophet inclines toward an expectation or desire, Satan will be there to add suspicion into his thoughts. Divine Revelations, however, are the commands of God. This means that the attributes of *isma* (infallibility) and *yaqin* (certitude of truth) in Prophets are connected to Divine Revelation. Otherwise, making one's own decisions can create the possibility of error."[52] The Prophet's heart was full of

Divine love, and there were no barriers between him and God's commandments. Although this was the case, God still made him aware of the possibility of deception: *"Beware of them lest they tempt you away from any part of what God has sent down to you"* (Maeda 5:49). Perhaps God was preparing His Messenger for possible sedition. Maybe this is why the noble Prophet stated, "Perhaps my heart may also become clouded. This is why I repent one hundred times a day asking for God's forgiveness."[53] It is possible that he was expressing his concern about making a mistake. An issue which is a possibility even for a Prophet should be of major concern for the rest of us. This is why the noble Prophet approached the matter very seriously and frequently warned his followers.

Sometimes the human mind becomes preoccupied with the most unpleasant and absurd thoughts. On most occasions, it is difficult to prevent this. The best thing to do in such situations is to break the negative field formed by these thoughts, thus preventing their growth in the conscience. More importantly, one should avoid reflecting this inner struggle externally in order to avert its effect in the flow of life. The noble Messenger states, "God forgives and disregards unpleasant thoughts which cross the minds of my followers, providing they do not talk about them or act upon them."[54]

Envy and jealousy

Envy is one of the hidden mechanisms which Satan frequently exploits. Envy is a desire for the departure of a gift which is possessed by another or a wish for possession of it by oneself. This way, one becomes more honorable than the other. According to Raghib al-Isfahani, "Envy is a desire for the eradication of a gift from a person who rightfully deserves it." The real meaning of envy is 'wishing for the eradication of a God-given gift or a virtue from another person.' It does not matter whether the gift is desired for oneself or not.[55] Those who feel envy can plot all sorts of diabolical plans and perpetrate unimaginable evil. This is why one should seek refuge in God from those who possess envy as one does from Satan.

There is also a contest which God encourages His servants to enter; it is a race to be honored with the gifts which *"no eye has beheld and no mind has imagined."*[56] Indeed, it is a race to gain the nobility of beholding God, attaining eternity by being righteous:

> The virtuous and godly ones will certainly be in (Gardens of) bounty and blessing; on thrones, looking round (at the blessings of Paradise). You will recognize on their faces the brightness of bliss. They will be served to drink pure wine under the seal (of Divine sanction and preservation). Its seal is a fragrance of musk. And to that (blessing of Paradise), then, let all those who aspire (to things of high value) aspire as if in a race (with each other). (Mutaffifin 83:22–26)

By means of this holy race, the feeling for leaping toward perfection, which exists in humankind as a potential, will be enhanced.

Satan's relation to envy and jealousy is explained in the words of Prophet Joseph's father, Jacob, in the Qur'an. Once, Joseph related a dream of his to his father. Prophet Jacob, who interpreted the dream, realized that his son would become a Prophet and said, *"Oh my son! Do not relate your dream to your brothers, lest they devise a scheme against you. For Satan is a manifest enemy to humankind (and can incite them to do such a thing)"* (Yusuf 12:5). With his words, he was pointing out the fact that Satan has the ability to sow the seeds of envy and jealousy in humans and these feelings can encourage them to commit all types of evil. These are the very feelings which caused the conflict between Adam's sons, resulting in one's death at the hands of the other.

INFESTATION OF THE HEART

Satan aims his arrows directly at the heart. His evil whispers of deception originate in the heart. There are two definitions of the word 'heart.' One is 'the unique organ which resembles a pine cone, situated in the left of the human chest.' The other one is 'a spiritual entity liable to His commands, subject to accountability and punishment.' It is the true identity of human reality. Humanity has yet to solve the connection between the body and the heart in this sense.[57]

The Messenger of God draws our attention to the significance of the heart in the human body, "Verily! There is a morsel of flesh in the human body. When it is healthy, the entire body will also be in good health. However, if it inclines to duplicity, the rest of the body will gradually putrefy. Verily, this is the heart!"[58] Truly, the heart is the hardest entity to cure in the event of an illness. If it is not protected against assaults coming from all directions, it can cause irreparable damage. This is why the Qur'an says, *"They entreat God, 'Our Lord, do not let our hearts swerve after You have guided us'"* (Imran 3:8). The noble Messenger also prayed each morning and night, emphasizing the importance of protection, "O God Who transforms all hearts, make my heart steady in Your religion."[59]

The heart is the home of the human spirit and the headquarters of worship. The heart is the source of a spiritual river where emotions flow in fine lines through the universe to God. Since it is a priceless gift, it has countless enemies attempting to change the course of its flow. From gloom to paganism, pride to arrogance, false expectations to greed, lust to lassitude, selfishness to passion for position, many enemies await and watch for weaknesses so that they may pounce.[60]

Our identity lies in the heart. This is why both perception and the perceiver are in it. Through it, I reach my intelligence, soul, free will, and body. Discernment is its view, intelligence is its soul, and free will is its power. We call this entity our 'heart.' This is why we frequently use phrases such as "I felt it in my heart," "I know it by heart," or "My heart is not in it." Sometimes we also refer to it to describe other qualities, such as 'heartsick' for cowards and 'heartless' or 'stone-hearted' for tyrants. It is also used for describing bravery and altruism; for example, we use the phrase, "He is all heart" to describe a brave, strong or a good-hearted person.[61]

The heart only finds peace when it senses proximity to God and feels that it is under His protection. This is when it is saved from the hazards of loneliness and confusion. It attains tranquility when it understands the reason for creation and the concept of the beginning and the end. The concept of attaining contentment through the remembrance of God is such a deep reality that only those who experience faith in their contented hearts may understand this. Words are not enough to explain this fact to those who do not know. This is a feeling that flows into the heart. With it, the heart finds peace. Contentment and security are truly felt. Only then does it realize that it is not alone and that those around it are all friends and allies simply because all that is around it is God's art, and therefore under His protection.[62]

However, there is no rule stating that all believing hearts will attain contentment. Satan pesters many faithful hearts, whispering evil into them in order to lead them astray. In relation to this, the following hadith is very significant: "Two of the Prophet's Companions, Abdullah ibn Abbas and Abdullah ibn Amr, ran into each other. Abdullah ibn Abbas asked, 'Which verse from the Book of God gives you the most hope?' He replied with the verse, '*O My servants who desecrate their souls (by using them in a wrong way) do not lose hope in God's mercy…*' Then, Abdullah ibn Abbas continued, 'For me it is the verse when Abraham said, "*O my Lord, show me how You resurrect the dead.' (God) asked, 'Did you not believe?' Abraham replied, 'I most certainly did. However, I wish to attain full contentment (by seeing).' God was pleased with Abraham's reply 'I certainly believe.'*" Abdullah ibn Abbas concluded by saying, 'Resurrection is an issue which Satan may exploit to whisper suspicion into people's mind.'"[63]

There are also hearts addicted to illness. "Illness is when a human being comes out of his or her natural disposition. There are two types of illnesses; one relates to the body, the other may be defined as ill-manners. The symptoms of the latter are ignorance, timidity, parsimony, hypocrisy, and similar traits."[64]

Yes, the purity and health of the heart is essential. Minds purified of suspicion, duplicity and rebellion against the Divine commands indicate a pure and sincere heart. It is quite difficult for those with diseased hearts to find the right path:

> Whoever God has willed to put to a trial (to prove his nature and has failed in this trial), you have no power in anything on his behalf against God. Such are those whose hearts (because of their rushing in unbelief) God does not will to purify. For them is disgrace in the world, and in the Hereafter a mighty punishment. (Maeda 5:41)

So, those who fail to maintain a pure and clean heart will always travel through the valleys of corruption.

There are also hearts which have been sealed. Belief in the unseen and knowledge of God is accomplished by sensing the essence of the heart. Those who sense the heart but ignore its invitation will continue to worship the materialistic idols which stand before their eyes. These are the hearts which have been sealed.

Hearts that constantly interact with sin resemble a tarnished mirror, unable to reflect, observe, feel, or sense. The noble Prophet stated, "When a believer commits a sin, a black spot appears on his heart. If he feels guilty and quickly repents, his heart transforms back into its luminous form. However, if he continues to sin, his heart continues to darken." This is the corrosion which God mentions in the Qur'an: *"But what they themselves have earned has rusted upon their hearts (and prevents them from perceiving the truth"* (Mutaffifin 83:14).

The heart is a target onto which arrows rain from all directions, it is a mirror that reflects many different shapes and figures, and it is a lake into which many different rivers flow. Yes, the heart is an entity that is continuously tugged and pulled from one side to another by both angels and satans. For this reason, whilst it has the potential to accommodate all good, it also possesses the ability to allow passage to evil whispers. The noble Messenger elucidates the issue, "The heart is under pressure from two directions. One is the angel, pledging good and endorsing the truth. Whoever feels this in his heart should know that it is from God, and so he should praise Him. The other pressure comes from the enemy (Satan), encouraging evil, denying the truth and holding back from good deeds. Whoever feels this, should seek refuge in God from Satan, the rejected." The noble Prophet then concluded by reciting the following verse: "*Satan frightens you with poverty and bids you into indecencies*" (Baqara 2:268).[65]

In conclusion, attaining a pure heart is the main objective of every Muslim. Working to achieve this goal is an imperative for a Muslim.

4

Satan's Exploitation of Worship

SATAN'S EXPLOITATION OF WORSHIP

Here are we on one side, struggling to worship God and to fulfill our responsibilities as servants, and on the other, there is Satan and his party working actively to lead us away from the straight path. On one hand, we are to defeat Satan and his party and, on the other, we have to overcome the difficulties of worship—no matter how small they are—to reach the horizons of true humanity. Here is the commandment of God:

> O humankind! Worship your Lord Who has created you as well as those before you (and brought you up in your human nature and identity), so that you attain reverent piety toward Him and His protection (against any kind of straying and its consequent punishment in this world and the Hereafter. (Baqara 2:21)

Against this, there is Satan with his party plotting thousands of diabolical schemes to destroy each person's eternal happiness. Then, there is the purpose of creation, which includes all these elements. Indeed, these are all realities. But no matter how great the task is, it is not impossible. Since the Almighty God does not overburden anyone, it seems that we are capable of fulfilling His commands.

Continuing our worship with dedication and devotion will support us on our holy path, since, "Just as a believer wears out his camel on a journey, he also drains the energy out of Satan with his prayers and worship, leaving him powerless."[1] This way, the influence of Satan on humans decreases, and his whispers become futile. In other words, as man worships, he protects himself from Satan, and when he protects himself from the evil one, he worships more and in awareness. Thus, worship results in distancing oneself from Satan, and staying away from Satan results in worship. This is a circle of reproduction.

However, the opposite scenario is also possible, where one shows negligence toward worship, failing to fulfill one's obligations to God. This in turn increases the pressure exerted by Satan, who gets the opportunity to whisper deception. We will eventually lose the battle unless we defy Satan with worship. Insisting on sins and abstaining from worship strengthens Satan, and so the situation will change into a vicious circle, trapping a person indefinitely. Neglecting worship means falling into the hands of Satan, and this in turn results in becoming his plaything. Almighty God issues the following warning:

> Would any of you wish to have a garden of palms and vines with rivers flowing in it, where he has all kinds of crops, and that, when old age has come upon him while he still has offspring too small (to look after their affairs), a fiery whirlwind should smite it and it should be burnt up? Thus does God make clear to you the Revelations (and signs of truth), that you may reflect on them (and act accordingly). (Baqara 2:266)

One day, Caliph Umar recited this verse to his friends and asked, "What do you think about this verse?" They replied, "God knows best." Umar was not pleased and said, "Why don't you reply by saying either you know or you don't." Upon this, Ibn Abbas said, "O Caliph of believers! I have some knowledge regarding this verse." Umar replied, "The son of my brother, do not be humble—tell us what you know." Ibn Abbas said, "It is an example given in relation to a deed." Umar asked, "What deed?" Abbas replied, "A particular deed." Then Umar explained, "It is about a wealthy man who worshipped the Almighty, All-Powerful God, in total obedience. Then, God sent him a devil. The man then dived into sins. Then, God diminished all of his good deeds."[2]

The time of worship is the period in which Satan launches his heaviest assaults on human beings. Looking at the issue from this angle, human beings try to carry out the principles of worship properly, while they are forced to engage in a struggle with Satan. Those who succeed are living their lives in accordance with the purpose of creation.

PRAYERS (*SALAT*)

Salat is the most important worship performed in the name of servanthood to God. Faith and the five daily prayers are like twins. They are very close and resemble each other. Satan was tested with prostration, which is part of the prayer, but he failed by opposing the command.

What is essential in worship is to catch the spirit of all the different compulsory moves and actions performed. It is an effort to attain the essence of worship by respectfully acknowledging that we are His servants. Prayers and worship should not be transformed into folkloric movements, and spirit must not be sacrificed to formalities. Comprehending the essence of *ihsan* should be the main objective. As the noble Messenger defines it, "*Ihsan* is worshipping God as if you were observing Him. Although you are unable to see Him, He sees you, because He is the All-Seeing."[3] Only then is the true essence of worship comprehended, and thus the phase of complete prayers has commenced. One who attains such a level performs his prayers as if he were drinking spiritual honey; meanwhile, there will be one experiencing the agony of depression and disillusionment elsewhere, and that is Satan. The noble Messenger states, "When the children of Adam recite the *sajda* (prostration) verse and prostrate, Satan moves into a corner, begins to weep, and then he says, 'Woe to me! God commands man to bow down, and thus he obeys. (He is victorious.) Paradise awaits him. Whereas I was also commanded to bow down, but I refused and rebelled. My fate is fire.'"[4] Although Satan appears to be regretful, he has never taken a step back or repented for his wrongful acts. On the contrary, he continues to harass those who obey God's commandments and works relentlessly to make rebels of them.

Satan uses one of his most powerful weapons, whispers of suspicion, during the performance of ritual ablution (*wudu*). Those
who are apprehensive wash their hands and feet over and over
again. One hadith warns us about an evil one by the name of
'Walahan' who uses ablution water to whisper doubts.[5] Scruples
also result in wasting water. The noble Prophet states, "There is no
virtue in using excessive water during ablution because this is from
Satan."[6] The whispers of deception in relation to ablution continue
during the performance of the prayers. Satan influences one to sup-
pose that one's ablution is broken. This in turn causes one to doubt
the authenticity of the prayer. Therefore, all concentration is lost
due to scruples. This is exactly what Satan wants. The noble
Messenger said, "When one of you begins to perform his prayer, a
satan comes and captures him as one would capture prey. Then,
you experience a sensation as if you had broken wind. In such a situation, unless you hear a sound or detect an odor, do not break
your prayer and do not doubt."[7] There are many similar hadiths
instructing us not to abandon prayers unless a sound is heard or an
odor is detected.[8]

The prayer shatters the constricted dimensions encircling us and
enables us to sail toward eternity. One becomes closest to God during prayer and at the moment of prostration. This is why the noble
Prophet said, "Prostration is the time when one becomes closest to
God; therefore, offer your prayers in abundance during prostration."
Performing prayers, which is a sign of being close to God, restrains
one from committing sins and acts of evil: *"Establish the Prayer in
conformity with its conditions. Surely, the Prayer restrains from all that is
indecent and shameful, and all that is evil"* (Ankabut 29:45).

Those who perform their prayers in a proper manner will enter
an atmosphere of being close to God for the rest of the day. As they
are confronted by temptation, the pressure applied by their consciences will restrain them. Satan becomes extremely agitated by all
of this. That is why he never leaves us alone during a prayer. The
noble Messenger states, "When *adhan* is called, Satan turns his back

and flees from the scene. He returns upon the completion of *adhan* but flees once again during *qamat*. Then, he comes back again to whisper deception into one's heart. He says, 'Remember this and remember that.' Then, one begins to dither, thinking 'Did I perform four cycles of prayer or three?' If any of you hesitates about the number of cycles performed, let him offer a *sajda al-sahw (prostrations of forgetfulness).*"[9]

Satan also approaches those who perform their prayers in congregation. If he finds a gap between them, he squeezes in to harass them. The noble Messenger also warns us about this, "Keep your lines tight because Satan fills the gaps."[10] In another hadith, the noble Prophet says, "Keep your lines solid, straighten the shoulders and fill the gaps. Be kind to your brothers, (if someone wishes to join the congregation, ease your shoulders so that he may pass through). Do not leave gaps for Satan to fill. Whoever fills a gap in the line will attract God's mercy. Whoever causes a break in the lines, God will break ties with him."[11]

Performing prayers symbolizes one's submission to God. Therefore, the prayers should be performed with extreme care and total respect. The prayer performed with care will diminish the opportunities which Satan hopes to obtain during the prayer. For this reason, a well performed prayer is one of Satan's greatest hates. He approaches human beings during prayers, reminding them of irrelevant matters in order to break their concentration. He tries to push them into useless thoughts and feelings. When tranquility is removed from the heart and the worshipper begins to focus his attention on things around him, Satan has stolen something from his prayer. Aisha explains, "I asked the Prophet about turning the head to glance around during a prayer. He replied, 'That is Satan thieving from your prayers.'"[12] Turning your head to look around during a prayer means Satan has succeeded in preoccupying you with other issues. Those in such situations either fail to remember or peace has abandoned their hearts. According to Islamic principles of practice, this is reprehensible (*makruh*). Husayn at-Tiybi explains, "Looking around during the prayer is an indication that tranquility has left the heart. Since it is an unpleasant thing to do, it was described as 'Satan thieving from one's prayer.' During the performance of the prayer, one implores and seeks refuge in his Lord. Since his heart has turned toward his Lord, He also turns toward Him. At that instant, Satan waits in a crouching position, ready to pounce. As soon as the worshipper turns his head around, the opportunity has risen for Satan to take as much as he can." According to Ibn Baziza, "Turning one's head around during a prayer is related to Satan because it breaks the momentum of spiritual connection with God."[13]

A hadith qudsi explains the spiritual connection and interaction which occurs between God and the worshipper during a prayer. Abu Hurayra heard the Prophet say, "God said, 'I have divided the prayer into two halves. One half belongs to Me and the other to My servant.' When His servant says, 'All praise and gratitude are for God, the Lord of the worlds,' God replies, 'My servant praised Me.' When His servant says, 'The All-Merciful, the All-Compassionate,' God says, 'My servant exalted Me.' Then when His servant says, '(He is the) Master of the Day of Judgment,' God says, 'My servant has exalted Me; this half is Mine.' When His servant says, 'You alone do we worship and from You alone do we seek help,' God replies, 'This is between me and My servant.' Finally, when His servant says, 'Guide us to the Straight Path, the Path of those whom You have favored, not of those who have incurred (Your) wrath, nor of those who are astray,' God answers, 'This belongs to My servant; there is everything for My servant who seeks.'"[14]

Such a bond is formed when the prayer is performed in perfection that Satan will not rest upon seeing man achieve such a high level. Hence, he pesters everyone who stands for the prayer. On one occasion, he even tried to disturb the noble Prophet. Abu Hurayra narrates, "God's Messenger said, 'Last night Satan attempted to distract me so that I may break my prayer. However, God granted me victory over him.'"[15] One of the Prophet's Companions, Abu Rawh explains, "One day, we performed a prayer led by God's Messenger. During the prayer, God's Messenger recited *Surat al-Rum*. He was distracted in some parts of the recitation. When the prayer concluded, he said, 'Some of you came to pray without *wudu* (they did not take ablution appropriately). For this reason Satan caused a stir. Make sure you perform your *wudu* appropriately before attending the prayer.'"[16]

Yes, young or old, Satan approaches all those who pray, with the intention to strike and paralyze their religious lives. His campaign of destruction continues during the *tasbihat* which follows the prayer. The Prophet said, "There are two qualities which will take one into Paradise if one can only preserve them. Although they are quite easy to perform, unfortunately many fail to do so. Following each prayer, one recites *Subhanallah* ten times, *Alhamdulillah* ten times and *Allahu Akbar* ten times. Although, with the tongue, they total one hundred and fifty (as they are recited after each of the five daily prayers), on the *mizan* (grand scales of justice), their value is one thousand and five hundred. The second quality is repeating *Subhanallah* and *Alhamdulillah* thirty-three times, and *Allahu Akbar* thirty-four times upon entering your beds. The total number is one hundred. Yet, on the *mizan* it is worth a thousand." Abdullah ibn Amr says, "I saw God's Messenger counting with his hands." His Companions asked, "O God's Messenger, how could anyone refrain from such easy task?" He replied, "Satan comes at night and causes a person to fall asleep before he can recite them. Then, he comes back at prayer time. On completion, he reminds you of something you needed to do (and thus one stands up and leaves without reciting)."[17]

Satan is sinister in finding ways to keep us away from prayer. For example, when someone intends to get up and perform a prayer at night, Satan comes during his sleep: "When one of you is asleep, Satan ties three knots behind his neck. Then, he strokes each knot and says, 'Sleep, there is a long night ahead of you.' If the person wakes up and remembers God, one of the knots comes undone. Then, when he takes ablution, another knot comes undone. Finally, the third knot is undone as one stands before God to worship. From that point on, one reaches the morning in total joy, tranquility, and peace. The opposite is waking up as an indolent person whose heart is filled with blemish."[18]

Baydawi interprets Satan's knots as "an analogy which illustrates Satan's decoration of dreams and his efforts to encourage people to sleep more. The terminology is metaphorical. The three knots represents the prevention of three forms of worship. They are the remembrance of God, ablution and the prayers." Aliyy al-Qari explains the reason why the back of the neck was specified by the hadith, "This is the region of the brain which human beings utilize to enter into various fantasies and suspicions. Certainly, among all of our spiritual senses, this region is the most vulnerable to Satan's deception and trickery." Husayn at-Tiybi, on the other hand, interprets the knots as "Satan's influence to increase lethargy to make people feel as if they were unable to move."

Some liken Satan's knots to those used by people who are engaged in black magic.[19] Kamil Miras believes that there is a connection between these knots and black magic or witchcraft: "Black magic and witchcraft has been around since the beginning of history; thus, it left its negative marks on many tribes and civilizations in the past. It has become an issue from which we need to take refuge in God. It is all the more dangerous for ignorant hearts who cannot tell the difference between witchcraft and worship. The more surprising factor is that even in this modern century and within civilized nations, where science and knowledge have progressed so significantly, we see people who continue to perform or become influenced by this evil ancient practice. For this reason, those scholars were absolutely correct when they interpreted the 'knot' mentioned in this hadith by Abu Hurayra, as 'the knot upon the heart and a paralyzing effect experienced by free will and logic.' Apparently, Satan enters the mind of those who intend to perform the night supererogatory *tahajjud* prayer, preventing them from waking up by whispering, 'Sleep! There is a long night ahead of you.'"[20]

Those who wake up and perform their prayers contrary to Satan's aggravations should regard this as a gift from God. By performing a prayer, one has brightened one's dark night; hence, morning has been reached by pleasing God. The opposite can be described as falling prey to Satan's stratagem by displaying lethargy and indolence. In this case, one's conscience will be in distress due to failing to attain serenity. People described in the above hadith, "ones who sleep throughout the night without a prayer [and who] will awaken with darken hearts and displeased souls" are not those who intend to wake up for a night prayer but fail to do so. Those with pure intentions to wake up and worship their Lord will be rewarded by God as if they had prayed. The noble Messenger states, "If a believer goes to bed with the intention of performing the midnight prayer but fails to wake up, his sleep will be rewarded to him by God, as charity. At the same time, the intended prayer will be recorded in his book of deeds."[21] This is why one should go to bed with the intention of getting up to perform a prayer every night.

Besides tying knots at the back of people's necks to stop them from praying, Satan also urinates in their ears. One day, the Companions talked about a man who "always slept throughout the night and never broke his sleep to perform a prayer." Upon hearing this, the Prophet said, "Satan urinates in his ears."[22] Abu Jafar Tahawi explains, "What is intended here is the sleep that begins without the performance of *isha* (night prayer). The Prophet advised against sleeping before performing the night prayer because of the risk associated with missing the prayer. Abandoning a prayer contradicts God's command, and thus it makes Satan happy. The word 'urinated' means he has done the worst thing possible. The phrase is metaphorical, and it should be taken as an analogy. It does not mean Satan uses one's ear like a toilet bowl."[23] However, Qadi Iyad and Qurtubi took the meaning to be literal.[24]

Sometimes, we may go to bed early and later wake up to perform the night prayer. At times, we may perform the night prayer, but we wake up with the intention of performing the *tahajjud*. We also wake up before daybreak to perform the morning prayer. So, the sleep mentioned above is the one in which any of these prayers are abandoned. It is not important whether we take the meaning literally or metaphorically; what matters is that it points to the fact that Satan never leaves human beings alone. He tries to destroy us when we are asleep, awake, laughing, or crying.

The probability of missing the morning prayer is higher than of missing the night prayer. Most people go to bed after performing the night prayer. It is the morning prayer for which one needs to wake up and prepare. For this reason, special care needs to be taken. Abu Hurayra explains, "Returning from the battle of Khaybar, God's Messenger walked throughout the night. Then, when he felt sleepy, he decided to rest. He said to Bilal, 'Watch the night. (Do not fall asleep so you can wake us up for the morning prayer.)' God's Messenger and his Companions went to sleep as Bilal tried to occupy himself for a while. Towards the morning, Bilal leaned on his mount and gradually closed his eyelids. No one woke up until they felt the sun on their faces. God's Messenger was the first to wake up in shivers, 'O Bilal (what happened to you)!' Bilal replied, 'O God's Messenger, the thing that grabbed you has also grabbed me.' Then, God's Messenger said, 'Take your mounts and walk away because Satan is nearby.' Later he asked for water, he performed ablution and then led the morning prayer. Upon completion, he said, 'Whoever forgets to pray should perform it as soon as he remembers because God instructs, 'In order to remember Me, perform your prayers appropriately.'"[25] They were returning from a battle. Everyone was extremely fatigued. There were wounded among them. They had walked all night. Then the noble Messenger decided to give them a rest. He was concerned about the morning prayer because it was only a few hours before daybreak. He gave Bilal the duty of waking them up. Thus, he had taken all precautions. Yet, the prayer was still not performed on time, and the Prophet related this to Satan's doing. Yes, wherever there is an error, negligence, and a slip-up in relation to worship, you can be sure that Satan is involved, using all his faculties to bring humankind down.

Once, the noble Prophet performed a prayer wearing a silk shirt that he had received as a gift. Upon completion of the prayer, he took it off with a strong dislike (upon Archangel Gabriel's coming with the prohibition of wearing silk for men) and said, "This is not appropriate for God-fearing pious people."[26] By this, he was giving a message to us regarding the spirit of the prayer and the importance of abstaining from all that is not related to it. Respect for the Almighty has to be preserved at all cost.

Walking in front of a person when he is performing a prayer will probably distract him causing a loss of concentration. This is why the place of prayer must be carefully designated. Sometimes, praying in a place where people are likely to pass by cannot be avoided. In these situations, one must screen oneself. This is called *sutra*, which means 'to cover or to veil.' *Sutra* may be a person standing up or sitting down, or a creature such as a horse. "It is sufficient for a worshipper to use a garment or a book as *sutra* in front of him."[27] If one cannot find even a stick to place in front of him as *sutra*, then one should draw a line on the ground so as to focus one's concentration on a single spot. This way, one is not distracted by things which may take attention away from the prayer. *Sutra* also helps to keep attention on one place, preventing people from looking around.[28]

The noble Prophet stated, "When one of you is praying, do not let anyone pass in front of you. Try to stop him to the best of your ability. Confront him, if he resists because this is from Satan."[29] In another version of this hadith, the noble Prophet says, "Make sure you stand close to *sutra* when you pray, so that Satan does not intervene."[30] The term Satan related to those who walk in front of worshippers is figurative. It should be regarded as an analogy to describe the acts of a human being who has no idea about righteousness.[31] People attempting to do this should be stopped with a kind gesture. However, as the hadith suggests, if they do not comply, then a firmer approach may be necessary; hence, it should be used when there are no other alternatives. The reason for this is that such a person, who resists irrationally, can only be of a satanic nature. The noble Prophet likens stubbornness to Satan. In some cultures stubborn people are compared to Satan. "We know that hideous characters that have lost everything that stands for good from their nature, and have become a slave to evil by performing Satan's duties are also referred to as satans."[32]

Moreover, the noble Messenger suggests, "If any of you becomes suspicious of his prayer, he should quickly remove all doubts out of his head. Then, he should perform two extra *sajdah*s (prostrations of forgetfulness). If the prayer was correct, the two *sajdah*s become supererogatory prayer; however, if the prayer was inadequate, then the extra two *sajdah*s will make it complete. These extra two *sajdah*s rub Satan's nose on the ground."[33]

FASTING (*SAWM*)

The true meaning of worship is obedience. Muslims are people who through obedience look for ways to please their Creator and Sustainer, Who has blessed them with countless gifts. In contrast, Satan, who envies them, tries everything in his power to prevent this. To achieve his evil plot, not only does he interfere with the prayer, a form of worship which caused his downfall, but he also attempts to intervene in all aspect of religious life. He wishes to form mountains on the paths of believers. As he does with the prayer, he also tries to impede fasting.

Fasting is abstaining from eating, drinking, and sexual intercourse between the times of *imsaq* (before dawn) and sunset with the intention of worship.[34] In an ethical way, humanity needs fasting and should establish it as part of their regular lives. By means of this struggle, the carnal soul develops virtuous morals. The inclination toward bad deeds is controlled with fasting. Observing the fast breaks the passion for lust, minimizes the wishes of the carnal soul, and discredits worldly faults such as love for fame, rank, arrogance, superiority, and haughtiness. Hence, it increases the inclination of the heart toward God.

The two essences of lust, which causes all sorts of trouble to human beings, are the proclivity toward the opposite sex and the appetite of the stomach. The humanity of a human being is proportional to the level of control he or she has over these two desires. Fasting initially breaks these two desires, throwing them into indolence. Their control transforms into free will. Fasting provides so many benefits that a hadith Qudsi states, "Fasting is Mine, only I (God) will reward it."[35] Fasting is like a shield that defends soldiers in battle; it protects us from hellfire. Hell is surrounded by lust, just as Paradise is surrounded by things the carnal soul dislikes (such as controlling one's desires and worship). This means that if we can control carnal desires by fasting, we also protect ourselves from hellfire on the Day of Judgment. Fasting has this constructive quality about it.

The month of Ramadan has been reserved for fasting. The noble Prophet said, "When Ramadan comes, the gates of hell are shut, the gates of Paradise are opened, and satans are chained."[36] Qadi Iyad says, "The hadith may be taken literally; hence, factuality is probable. The opening of heaven's gates and closing of hell's gates is a sign of significance bestowed upon this month. The tying up of satans means they will be prevented from harassing the believers. We may also derive a metaphorical meaning such as the abundance of rewards and forgiveness. The deception and pestering of satans decreases so much that it is as if they were tied up, and their area of maneuver becomes restricted during the month of Ramadan. Their influence is limited to some entities and people. The phrase 'the gates of Paradise are opened' supports this view. We can interpret this as God opens the gates of blessings such as fasting, the *tarawih* prayers, charity and alms for the needy, and He protects His servants from various evil deeds. All of these constitute a way of entering Paradise."[37]

The "opening of heaven's gates" also means the doors of good deeds are kept open. It means that the Almighty is pleased and His approval has engulfed all. The closing of hell's gates, on the other hand, can be considered as meaning the hearts of those who fast are protected and provocations to sins and bad deeds have been blocked. With regard to the meaning of "Satans are chained," Aliyy al-Qari states, "It means that the aggressive evil ones are in chains; therefore, human hearts are closed to their deceptions and instigations. Man's inclination toward evil emotions, such as rage, diminishes with fasting. His sense of obedience and righteous logic is enhanced. These transformations are clearly observed during the month of Ramadan. As a matter of fact, Ramadan is the month in which sins are minimized and worship is in abundance."

Some may ask, "Why do some people continue to commit sins during Ramadan, if satans are in chains?" In regard to this, Badraddin al-Ayni stated in his annotated interpretation of Sahih Bukhari, "This applies to those who take care with the principles of fasting. As explained above, only the aggressive evil ones are chained. The meaning intended by this is that there is a significant reduction in sins committed due to their provocations. This is a unique quality of Ramadan. This is the month in which fewer sins occur compared to others."[38]

The term "Satans are chained" is interpreted by Halimi in this way: "It is possible that these are the satans who steal information from the angels in the heavens. It is probable that they are restrained during the nights of Ramadan. The reason for this is that they were banned from stealing information during the revelation of the Qur'an. This may also mean that their ability to deceive believers throughout the year is reduced during Ramadan. As Muslims become heavily engaged in activities such as reciting the Qur'an and remembering God, satans are disillusioned."[39]

Pilgrimage to Mecca (*Hajj*)

No matter where we go or in which time zone we live, Satan's intervention will never vanish. Assuming the opposite would mean that the mystery of the test is not valid in certain places or times, so this would be an incorrect assumption. Even if one were to sit before the Ka'ba or in the presence of the noble Messenger, Satan would still attempt to approach, looking for ways to whisper his deceptions. This is why, no matter where we are, we need to protect ourselves from his evil. If this were not the case, why would the Prophet seek refuge in God as he entered the Masjid? As human beings, we are compelled to exchange blows with Satan throughout our lives.

Nevertheless, the efforts of Satan and his party do become less effective in certain holy places. There is solid evidence that crime rates drop significantly during Ramadan. This means that there is a connection between the statistics and the phrase "the satans are chained." However, the mystery of the test will never diminish and humankind will not be deprived of free will or freedom of choice.

Humans are vulnerable to Satan's attacks even when they are encircling the Ka'ba or asking for forgiveness at Arafat. The *hajj* is a pilgrimage to a certain place, at a certain time, and a performance of certain duties. The certain place of the pilgrimage is the Ka'ba and the plains of Arafat, and the certain time of the pilgrimage is the lunar months of Shawwal, Dhu al-Qada and the first ten days of Dhu al-Hijja. There is also a time for each obligation. For *wuquf* (standing), the period begins at the daybreak on the day of Arafat and continues till the morning of the sacrificial Eid. Entering certain sacred places in the state of *ihram* with the intention to perform *hajj* is part of the process of worship.[40]

One of the necessities (*wajib*) of *hajj* is the stoning of Satan. Following the *tawaf* of visiting, people return to Mina and stay three days to cast pebbles at the Jamras. It is reprehensible (*makruh*) to stay elsewhere during the period of stoning. On the second day of

Eid, commencing at sunset, beginning from the first Jamra located next to the Masjid al-Hayf, pilgrims cast seven pebbles at each of the three Jamras. The same process is carried out on the third day of Eid.[41]

The noble Prophet explained an incident in relation to Divine Wisdom regarding the stoning of Satan. Archangel Gabriel took Abraham to the valley of Jamra al-Aqaba. Here, Satan appeared before him, and Abraham cast seven stones at him. Satan was buried in the earth by the force of the stones. Later, Abraham came to Jamra al-Wusta. Once again, Satan appeared and Abraham cast seven stones which buried him in the earth. When Abraham came to Jamra al-Kuswa, the same occurred.

Satan had also appeared to Abraham in human form when he was taking Ishmael to the place of sacrifice by the order of God. Satan tried to influence Abraham into disobeying the command. When he failed, he turned to Abraham's son. Satan could not persuade Ishmael either, so he went to Hagar. However, when he failed to convince Hagar, he departed filled with hatred and rancor.[42] Abraham's confrontation with Satan is not mythical, for he saw Archangel Gabriel, the informer of truth and good, and so he also saw the informer and the symbol of evil.

PRESCRIBED PURIFYING ALMS (*ZAKAT*)

Another form of worship which Satan tries to stop is *zakat*. In the dictionary this is defined as 'an increase or purification.' *Zakat* is the purification of wealth. There is also the term *tazkiya*, which is interpreted as 'the thing taken out of wealth so that it may be purified.' In the verse, *"He will indeed be successful who purifies it"* (Shams 91:9), *zakat* is used in its lexical meaning. In religious terminology *zakat* is 'the process of giving a certain percentage of your wealth to a certain party for the sake of God.' The 'certain percentage' described here is the amount of alms to be given, 'wealth' is the nominated amount possessed by the individual and 'the certain party' is the person or persons with rights to receive *zakat*.[43]

There is Divine Wisdom in giving *zakat*. It is a form of thanks to God for the wealth He has granted. It saves the carnal soul from the illness of parsimony. It encourages Muslims to be generous. It shrinks the social and economic gap which exists between people. It removes the desires which people have for the wealth of others. It fights poverty and famine. Therefore, *zakat* prevents the occurrence of many probable crimes. A starving individual is capable of committing all types of crime. This way, certain desires are kept under control.

Zakat means the returning of the rights of the poor which have been mixed into the wealth of the rich. According to scholars, it is a form of test applied to believers by God. Muslims believe in God, give their word to obey His every command and refrain from things He has forbidden. *Zakat* was established to test the loyalty of believers. A wealthy man who gives his *zakat* has kept his word and has successfully completed his test. Those who refuse to give alms display their love for wealth; hence, they fail the test and lose both in this world and in the one after.[44]

As in all forms of worship, we have to fight with the desires of our carnal soul and the whispers of Satan, when giving *zakat*. Acts of worship such as daily prayers and fasting are performed with the body. However, *zakat* is performed by giving a part of our wealth, which is considered to be the jewel of our life. For this reason, Satan has significant influence in this issue. He approaches those who are obliged to give *zakat*, threatening them with poverty: "*Satan frightens you with poverty and bids you into indecencies*" (Baqara 2:268). Not only does he obstruct the path of *zakat* and charity with threats of poverty, but he also encourages us to spend our money on things which God is displeased with.

Satan has lost all hope in God's mercy. Therefore, in order to foil all efforts at philanthropy, he contaminates the heart with bleakness and manipulative ideologies, threatening the carnal self with poverty. He commands ugliness by encouraging parsimony. He promotes lust, adultery, and rebellion so that people may waste their wealth on them.[45] The noble Prophet describes the form of charity which receives the highest reward, "When one feels healthy and desires wealth, when one feels miserly and afraid of becoming poor, and when one's mind is occupied with wealth, this is the time of charity. Do not delay (this) until such a time when you begin to say, 'I shall give this much to that person and that much to this person.' Beware; that money already belongs to someone."[46]

This means that *zakat* and charity become more virtuous when we have to deal with our carnal soul and struggle with Satan. Earning and collecting whilst in good health, proving oneself by succeeding in life and then giving charity is more rewarding. This is true philanthropy and a path encouraged by the Prophet. This is also a sign of trust in God and defeating Satan.

5

Means of Protection

Means of Protection

Generally, all good deeds are positive and constructive; all bad deeds are negative and destructive. Destruction is quite easy. Construction, however, is difficult. We all know that it takes months for many hardworking people to build a house, but a child with a box of matches can burn it down in minutes. Since Satan stands on the side of evil, he is destructive. Contemporary scholar Fethullah Gülen states that the best form of protection against Satan's evil is to be spiritually equipped by attaining inner and outer unity. According to him, this unity relates to consistency between one's heart and actions.[1] Here, we will analyze the means of protection from Satan in three sections.

Spiritual armor

Prayers

Prayers are a special form of worship which indicates one's closeness to God, and those who pray are rewarded according to their intentions. Worship is total obedience to God, and it is performed in awareness, with the body and soul, internally and externally. Worship is submission, and prayers are the highest level of respect and sincerity. Scholars define worship as the greatest form of respect and reverence. It means living a life that will please God without asking why or questioning the reason behind the Divine Wisdom.[2] "It is personal submission offered with intention of worship and rewarded by God—obedience displayed by the body and soul in total submission to God."[3] It is a sign of compliance and capitulation to God.[4]

Worship points to the bond which exists between man and the Infinite Power. Worship is the reason for creation. The verse "*I have not created the jinn and humankind but to (know and) worship Me (exclusively)*"[5] makes this absolutely clear. Worship is doing the things God is fond of only for His sake. As Elmalılı Hamdi Yazır explains, it is doing your best without questioning; this is called *taabbudi*, or performing the acts of worship in full submission only because they are the commands of God.

In a hadith qudsi, the noble Prophet explains, "(God says,) 'I will declare war on those who show hostility to My servants who believe and worship in sincerity. There is no better way of approaching Me than performing the obligations (*fard*) I have set upon My servants. My Servant continues to come closer by performing supererogatory acts of worship. Then, I shall love him. I shall then become the hearing ear, the observing eye, the touching hand and the walking feet of My servant. I shall grant what he asks of Me. I shall protect, if he seeks refuge in Me. I have never hesitated in any of My decisions, except when I take the life of a believer. Since My servants are not fond of death, I am also not fond of something that gives pain to My servants.'"[6] God uses the phrase 'My servants' to embrace those who worship Him.

Performing supererogatory prayers along with the obligatory ones attracts God's love. It is not possible for those who are loved by God to fall into the traps set by Satan. Since God favors a worshipper and protects him from evil, this person will observe the truth and follow the path of righteousness. Satan cannot influence a genuine servant of God. This reality slipped out of Satan's own mouth:

> Iblis said, "My Lord! Because You have allowed me to rebel and go astray, I will indeed deck out to be appealing to them on the earth (the worldly , material dimension of human existence and the path of error), and I will surely cause them all to rebel and go astray, except Your servants from among them, endowed with sincerity in faith and Your worship." (Hijr 15:39–40)

Then, God said, "*This (path of sincerity in faith) is a straight path that I have taken upon Myself (to lead to Me). My servants you shall have no authority over any of them, unless it be such as follow you being rebellious (against Me, as you are)*" (Hijr 15:41–42).

It is obvious that it is not easy to achieve such a level of sincerity. Attaining it depends on sacrifice, struggle and relentless effort. However, even a small step toward this noble cause will make the task more achievable. The reason for this is that such a step becomes an invitation to God's aid. In relation to this, God says, "If My servant comes a hand closer to Me, I will come a yard closer to him. If He comes a yard closer to Me, I come two arms' length closer to him. If he walks toward Me, I run toward him."[7] The Almighty uses analogies to explain the fact that His help will be in abundance even for those who show a small effort. This is a law established by the Almighty. Whether they are made for success in this world or for the one after, all efforts will be supported by God depending on how we use our free will and prove ourselves. This way, we shield ourselves by seeking refuge in God and protecting ourselves from Satan's deceptions.

Reciting the Qur'an

The Qur'an can be defined as "the miraculous Divine Word revealed to Prophet Muhammad, upon whom be peace and blessings, written down on sheets and transmitted from the Prophet to the succeeding generations via numerous reliable channels, and which is used for worship by means of recitation."[8] God explains in His Divine Words, "*O humankind! There has come to you an instruction from your Lord, and a cure for what (of sickness or of doubt) is in the breasts, and guidance and mercy for the believers*" (Yunus 10:57). According to this verse, the Qur'an is an admonition, warning humanity against wickedness and evil; it is a remedy which cures all physical and spiritual illnesses; it is a guide showing people the straight path which leads to salvation; it is mercy which stands greater than wrath and attracts

God's mercy, pardoning and forgiveness when recited, comprehended, followed, and passed on to others.

These interpretations are expressed clearly in the following verse: "*We are sending down the Qur'an in parts—it is a healing and a mercy for the believers*" (Isra 17:82). This verse suggests that the world is like a hospital filled with all types of ailments, the noble Prophet is the doctor, and the Qur'an is the remedy. There is no doubt that the Qur'an is the best medicine for illnesses such as suspicion, hypocrisy, paganism, greed, despair, ignorance, indolence, evil intentions, imitation, extremism, and other social and psychological disorders. Moreover, there are also solutions to many physical problems which science has not discovered yet. However, these are all for believers; hence, the Qur'an will only increase the anguish of tyrants.[9]

One of the Prophet's wise Companions, Abdullah ibn Masud, said, "The Qur'an is a feast provided by God, so benefit as much as you can. This Qur'an is the rope of God; it is the light and a remedy (to all illnesses). It protects those who hold on, saves and pleases those who follow. Its originality is infinite. It does not wear out with applications. Read it for its recitation earns you rewards."[10] Abu Hurayra states, "A house in which the Qur'an is recited will expand. Angels will attend and Satan will flee from such a blessed dwelling. A house in which the Qur'an is not recited will shrink. Angels will leave and Satan will be present, causing a decrease in blessings."[11] If the Qur'an supplies such blessings to the house in which it is recited, then one can imagine the benefits to those who follow its path and who also encourage others to do so.

The noble Prophet stated, "Do not transform your homes into graveyards. Certainly, Satan flees from the house in which the *Surah Baqara* is recited."[12] Numan ibn Bashr transmits, "God's Messenger said, 'Satan will approach a house in which *Aman'r-rasulu* is not recited for three days.'"[13]

Once, the Companions of the Prophet went on a journey. Along the way, they came across a tribe whose chieftain had been bitten by a poisonous snake. One of the Companions recited *Surah Fatiha* and blew on the wound. The chieftain's health was restored.[14]

Satan uses many ways to approach humankind. He wishes to lead humans astray with different strategies. He whispers into their chest. He forms a barrier before good deeds. He decorates and then presents all evil deeds as if they were attractive acts. By various diabolical schemes, he tries to push the soul and the heart into despondency, dragging people into stress and dark desires. We are created for eternity, and therefore our hearts will never be satisfied by following Satan's path. Since we can never fulfill all of our desires, on Satan's path we will face ongoing psychological problems. This is when the Qur'an comes to our aid, answering our yearning for eternity. It whispers in our ear, "What you seek here, you will receive on the other side." The Qur'an fills the soul with tranquility and content. It transforms this life and the one after into peace and joy. In contrast to Satan's deceptions, the Qur'an promises happiness in both worlds, and by the permission of God it becomes a remedy for humankind's physical and spiritual ailments.

Piety and avoiding disobedience to God (Taqwa)

In a semantic sense, *taqwa* means 'to preserve and safeguard an entity from detrimental and harmful things by taking it under one's protection.' *Taqwa* is 'protection from and guarding against the things one fears.' This is why *taqwa* and *khawf* (fear) have been used interchangeably. In religious terminology, *taqwa* is defined as 'protecting oneself from things which may lead to sin, even things which are doubtful.' This includes staying away even from those things or acts that are *mubah* (i.e., neither commanded nor forbidden by religious law).[15]

The Lord's most favored quality is *taqwa*, and His most pure, distinguished servants are the God-revering, pious ones. The Qur'an is the purest form of message given in the name of *taqwa*. The Lord's great servants are nourished with the holy Qur'an here and with the blessings and good pleasure of the Owner of Infinite Mercy in the other world. The pleasure attained here and the spiritual joy there are Divine presents that are of secondary nature next to the depth of *taqwa*. Therefore, the Almighty reminds us of the importance of *taqwa*, *"Keep from disobedience to God in reverent piety with all the reverence that is due to Him"* (Imran 3:102). *Taqwa* means utilizing all possible means for performing good and closing all doors to evil, or trying to keep them closed, to the best of one's ability. Through *taqwa*, humankind avoids falling into the deepest pits and becomes a traveler on the path to *a'la-yi illiyin* (the highest possible rank). Thus, we could say that whoever finds *taqwa* has also found the source of all blessings, prosperity, and opulence.[16]

Khawf, or 'fear,' is the emotion felt because of concern about possible danger or harm. *Taqwa*, on the other hand, is removing the possibility of experiencing the concern or minimizing it with precaution.

To attain genuine *taqwa*, one must first have faith in God and then augment that faith. Faith (*iman*) means 'acknowledging the oneness of God with the heart and testifying to this with the tongue.'[17] The augmentation of faith can only be obtained by performing all religious obligations and refraining from major sins. The following verses describe the main principles of taqwa: *"those who believe and do good, righteous deeds,"* (Yunus 10:9) and *"those who avoid the major sins and indecent, shameful deeds"* (Shura 42:37).

Besides these, there is also *sagha'ir*, which means 'minor sins.' One should also tackle those in a serious manner. Complete *taqwa* can only be achieved by abstaining from what is *mubah*—those things tolerated by religious law. The noble Prophet states, "A believer cannot obtain *taqwa* unless he refrains from the tolerated things due to suspicion."[18]

To obtain *taqwa*, one needs to have adequate knowledge regarding forbidden activities such as sins and dangerous traps, and to have a certain amount of knowledge of God. This knowledge will entail respect for God. This is a dimension of *taqwa*, and it is called *khashyat*, or 'fear of God.' The verse, *"Of all His servants, only those possessed of true knowledge stand in awe of God,"* (Fatir 35:28) illustrates this lucidly. Knowledge of God, wisdom regarding what is lawful and unlawful, and refraining from what is forbidden constitute the three levels of genuine *taqwa*. As a matter of fact, the existence of one requires the existence of the others: one who knows God will learn His commands and prohibitions; therefore, he or she will show great effort to perform them, and his or her endeavors will bring about *taqwa*. As the Qur'an explains, *"Surely, the noblest, most honorable of you in God's sight is the one best in piety, righteousness, and reverence for God"* (Hujurat 49:13). God favors those who are God-fearing and pious.

Those living their lives as satellites of *taqwa* will avoid falling into traps laid by Satan because of the level of life they experience, just as a prayer performed with perfection protects the one who prays from making grave mistakes. The following verse explains this: *"Those who keep from disobedience to God in reverence for Him and piety—when a suggestion from Satan touches them, they are alert and remember God, and then they have clear discernment."* (A'raf 7:201). In such situations, those with *taqwa* control themselves and think of where they have gone wrong. Then, they detect Satan's deception and quickly take refuge in God.

People who do not lead such lives are disadvantaged. At any time Satan can easily deceive and lead them astray. They then follow his path, becoming his brothers: *"Whereas their brothers (the brothers of the satans in the form of human beings)—satans draw them deeper into error and do not relax in their efforts"* (A'raf 7:202).

Those who are advanced in *taqwa* are the best defenders against Satan's deception. God increases their rank for the victory they accomplish against him. The *taqwa* derived from the Qur'an is the shield of Muslims against Satan, their bunker is living a life prescribed by the noble Prophet, and their weapons are prayer, repentance, and seeking refuge in God.[19]

Doing good uninterruptedly

Predominantly, Satan attacks lethargic human beings. He pesters those who do not work, do not participate in religious activities, or do not renew themselves in the name of religion. Tackling the issue from this perspective, we need first of all to seek ways to be active.

Since Satan utilizes our indolence, encourages us to develop evil desires and commands us to commit bad deeds in our free time, we should then defend ourselves by engaging in spiritual activities more often. This way, we get a chance to retaliate and fill the gaps through which he plans to attack. Moreover, we need to be spiritually and physically equipped from tip to toe, so that we leave no room for a possible attack. A human being who contemplates his or her own creation and ponders on the creation of everything else, engages in inner and outer meditations, and constantly renews his or her interaction with God will—by the will of God—not be deceived by Satan's whispers of deception. Satan cannot dominate a person of dedication who works day and night for the sake of spreading God's name and religion all over the world.

The cursed hand of Satan cannot reach an individual whose heart has found contentment with *yaqin* (certainty and firm belief) because this heart is the source of Divine inspirations. Therefore, if we preserve strong ties with our Lord, then He will not leave us in the hands of His enemy, Satan. Would the Almighty thrust aside the efforts of a believer who submits to Him with loyalty by shouldering His religion? He is the most loyal and the most reliable; therefore, He will not leave us all alone to perish with our desires. Indeed, in His book He commands, *"fulfill My covenant (which I made with you through your Prophets) so that I fulfill your covenant"* (Baqara 2:40). Since this is so, would God leave us in the hands of Satan when we unremittingly work for His religion? This is unthinkable! On the contrary, He will manifest a verse on our tongues, drawing us toward Himself to protect us from the abyss formed by Satan, as He protected the wise Companions of the noble Messenger. Yes, there were times when even their visions were blurred because they were only human. However, the Almighty quickly manifested a proof before their eyes, turning their attention toward the eternal life.

If all those who serve the cause of God take a moment to reflect on their lives, they will see that whenever they attempt to use their free will for the wrong reasons or whenever a slip-up occurs, the hand of grace is there to protect them. Each of us must have clearly seen His helping hand reaching to us, depending on the level of our sincerity and loyalty. Yes, we must have all observed the manifestation of the mystery upon the face of free will: *"O you who believe! If you help God('s cause by striving in His cause), He will help you and make your feet firm"* (Muhammad 47:7).

Our free will is so limited that its frame is almost invisible. However, God recognizes it as a basic condition and disembowels all of Satan's violations. The desires of the carnal soul and Satan's influence are blocked with free will, and an opportunity for defense is provided. This point can be comprehended more clearly if we contemplate the times when the pressure of our desires becomes unbearable, or on the occasions when we defeat them even though we may have surrendered for a brief period of time. There are times and places in which the dynamism of our hearts may not be sufficient to keep us alert and wary. However, there are those whose faces reflect the truth, and God's will is manifested in their free will. This is so apparent that when you sit with them your spirit strengthens as if you were sitting beside the Prophet. Their words become an elixir, melting away evil desires and thoughts. Sometimes, we also evince this sensation and atmosphere. Then, others come to lean on us in order to maintain their existence.

God created human beings with a nature which is suited to social existence. Then, He placed us in society. People can only live out their spiritual and physical life in a society that thinks like they do. So, we should interact with righteous friends, since a righteous friend can at any time bring our hearts to life with laudable advice and recommendations. Such friendship should be preserved and maintained everywhere: on a journey, on social occasions and even on the way to the market. This type of vacuum or insulating friendship will act as a shield preventing satans from entering our circle.[20]

Being open to advice

In relation to advice, Fethullah Gülen says that, as frequently as possible, one should lend an ear to recommendations that soften the heart. Yes, advice which enables us to unite with our eternity and encourages enthusiasm and longing for everlasting life is absolutely vital. In this sense, religion is nothing other than advice. When our predecessors offered their sermons, mosques were filled with love and excitement. Although the great Fakhruddun Razi was a man who had virtually memorized all the books of learning, when he climbed the pulpit, his words could hardly be understood due to his loud weeping. Unfortunately, we are a community deprived of such talented scholars. Yet, human beings also need their hearts to jump with excitement whilst tears overflow from their eyes. Yes, in relation to their inner world, it is necessary for human beings to feel sensitive a few times a day, delving deep into their own souls. Weeping is a necessity. When the Qur'an mentions softened hearts, it says, "*And they fall down on their faces weeping*" (Isra 17:109). So, if possible, before we even set foot outdoors, every day we need to study at least a few pages and contemplate the lives of those who lived according to Islam, such as the Companions and those coming after them. This way our spiritual world will recover little by little, and so we will have the chance to compare ourselves to those people of the heart. I believe that, with comparisons such as "They were Muslims, and so are we; how did they became like that, and why are we like this?", we can establish self-accounting and spiritual renewal. This heart-softening process, even if it is only carried out a few times a week, will clear the rust from our inner worlds. Therefore, we will sense the Divine reflections in our hearts, distancing ourselves from the whispers of Satan.

This may also be brought about by listening to someone, reciting the Qur'an, or studying the commentaries. There are no limits to self-renewal, and we need it as we need air and water. Listening to a person who excites our hearts; sitting beside him and saying, "Give us advice;" feeling the presence of the noble Messenger and his loyal Companions in our hearts: these are the dynamics which will keep us on our feet.

Do not ever say, in a bored manner or out of familiarity, "I know all this, so what use if I read it again?" Arguing, "What difference does it make if I listen to these again" is heedlessness and a sign of being deceived. As the physical necessities of life, such as eating and drinking, recur, the components of our spiritual life such as the heart, conscience, and other emotions also need repeated spiritual nourishment.

With all this in mind, we should throw ourselves into the arms of a guide and look for ways to renew ourselves by entering into a divine atmosphere. Sometimes, this can be achieved by reading, contemplating, or reflecting on death. We will then be protected from both human and jinn satans, depending on the level of our success. Our prayers and pleas should always be directed at asking the Almighty to protect us from the desires of our carnal soul and from the evil deceptions of Satan, so that we may continue our lives in the mansions of Divine Grace.[21]

SEEKING REFUGE IN GOD

When we talk about protection from Satan, the first thing that comes to mind is seeking refuge in God. The Qur'an emphasizes the importance of the issue in two places by directly addressing the Prophet, *"And if a prompting from Satan should cause you hurt (as you carry out your mission or during worship or in your everyday life), seek refuge in God. He is All-Seeing, All-Knowing."*[22] The importance of seeking refuge in God is also demonstrated in the verse, *"And say, 'My Lord! I seek refuge in You from the promptings and provocations of the satans. I seek refuge in You, O my Lord, lest they be present with me'"* (Mu'minun 23:97–98).

The religious term for seeking refuge in God is *istiadha*. In the dictionary, this is defined as 'taking refuge in someone by going under his protection.' In religious terms it means 'to take refuge in God from Satan's evil by reciting *"A'udhu bi'llahi min ash-shaytani'r-rajim."*"[23] *Istiadha* is defined as 'asking for God's protection by using the word *a'udhu*.'

The holy Qur'an uses different terms in various places regarding seeking refuge in God: *"The Pharaoh (said to his chiefs), 'Let me kill Moses and let him call upon his Lord!'"* and Moses responded, *"Indeed, I seek refuge in my Lord Who is your Lord as well, from every haughty one who disbelieves in the Day of Reckoning!"* (Mumin 40:26–27). Haughtiness or arrogance is the most effective weapon used by Satan. This is why we need to take refuge in God from arrogance and the arrogant: *"Those who dispute concerning the signs and Revelations of God without any authority that has reached them, (do so because) in their bosoms is a craving for superiority, which they will not attain. But take refuge in God (from their schemes). Surely He is the All-Hearing, the All-Seeing"* (Mumin 40:56).

In relation to seeking refuge in God, Bediüzzaman Said Nursi provides the following explanation:

> Satans have no power or authority over creation in the universe. God always sides with the righteous, using His mercy and Grace. Also, the attractive beauty of the truth and reality encourages and confirms the righteous. In addition, the ugliness of corruption awakens abhorrence toward the wicked. In spite of all these, Satan and his team succeed on many occasions; therefore, the righteous always take refuge in God. The reason for this is evil and corruption is negative, destructive, nothingness, and disparaging. On the other hand, the way of the righteous and virtuous is positive, constructive, existent, and productive. It is quite evident that a house built by twenty men in twenty

days can easily be pulled down by a man in a day. Yes, a human body develops, exists, and survives by the laws of physics and life. Although it belongs to the power of the Almighty Creator, a tyrant condemns it to death—which is nonexistence if compared to life—by amputating one of its organs. This is why the phrase "Destruction is easy" became a catchphrase.

This is the secret behind the reason why sometimes the wicked proclaim victory over the powerful righteous by using really feeble effort. However, the righteous have a fortress so strong that if they utilize it as shelter, the relentless enemy can never approach or defeat them. Even if they inflict an insignificant amount of damage, with the secret of "happy ending belongs to the righteous," this damage can be restored by an eternal reward and benefit. This strong fortress and stronghold is the religion brought by Prophet Muhammad and his Sunna.

A question such as this may cross one's mind: The creation of satans who are comprised of pure evil and cause many people to go astray and enter into hellfire seems quite dreadful and gruesome. How could the mercy and grace of Almighty God, Who is the All-Gracious, the All-Compassionate, and the All-Merciful allow or permit the occurrence of such a thing? This is a question asked by many.

The question may be addressed with the following answer: Along with small and insignificant evil which subsists in the existence of Satan, there are many huge and complete reasons of good, and means which carry humankind to perfection. Yes, within the abilities of man's nature, there are many more levels than those that exist between a seed and a fully grown tree. Perhaps the levels are as many as those from an atom to the sun. Certainly, a procedure and interaction is essential for the development of these abilities. The cogwheel of development in this process can only be placed in motion or activated by combat. This combat can only occur if evil and Satan exist. Otherwise, the rank of humankind would have remained fixed, just as the angels, and thus thousands of levels and degrees would not exist...Abandoning thousands of virtues and good, to prevent the occurrence of one evil, contradicts Divine Wisdom and Justice.

It is true that many people fall into evil because of Satan. However, in most cases, worth and value is not measured by quantity, it is measured by ability and quality. Just as when a farmer plants thousands of seeds into the soil and, following a chemical process which occurs beneath the ground, he gets ten trees in return. The rest of the seeds have putrefied and perished. Obviously the benefits he would receive from the ten trees will by far cover the loss imposed by the perished seeds. Like the example, as a result of combating with the carnal soul and satans, the development of ten individuals of perfection who illuminate humanity, like the stars in the heavens, is a great benefit, honor and value. Certainly, this damage inflicted on the wicked—leading them astray—by a being that has less value than pests is so insignificant that Divine Mercy, Wisdom, and Justice have permitted the existence and influence of Satan.[24]

Ignorance is another factor which makes Satan's work easy, and so we are also instructed to protect ourselves from it, *"And remember Moses said to his people, 'God commands you to sacrifice a cow.' They responded, 'Are you making fun of us?' He replied, 'I seek refuge in God lest I should be among the ignorant (by making fun of anybody)'"* (Baqara 2:67). At the time of the Flood, Noah pleaded with God to spare his son from drowning. God replied, *"'O Noah! He (being an unbeliever) is not of your family. He is one of unrighteous conduct (which embodied his unbelief). So do not ask of Me what you have no knowledge of! I admonish you, so that you do not behave as one among the ignorant!' Noah said, 'O my Lord! I seek refuge in You, lest I should ask of You what I have no knowledge of. And unless You forgive me and have mercy on me, I will indeed be among the losers!'"* (Hud 11:46–47). With his reply, Noah was taking refuge in God from ignorance.

When a woman tried to seduce Prophet Joseph, he was frightened and asked for God's protection.[25] In order to keep his brother Benjamin next to him, he decided on a solution against his other brothers; and with the fear of doing something wrong, he sought protection in God.[26]

In these examples the protection of God was sought from arrogance, ignorance, and tyranny. It is clear that these qualities are the weapons of Satan, so it is imperative that one should take refuge in God from all of these acts.

When the wife of Imran gave birth to a girl child, she said, "*I have named her Mary and commend her and her offspring to You for protection from Satan, eternally rejected (from God's Mercy)*" (Imran 3:36). Also, when Mary beheld Angel Gabriel in human form, she said, "*I seek refuge in the All-Merciful from you, if you are a pious, God-revering one*" (Maryam 19:18).

As mentioned previously, God's Messenger was also required to seek refuge in God, and in relation to this he was addressed directly in two verses. The surahs *Falaq* and *Nas* are known as *Mu'awwidhatayn*. When *Surah Ikhlas* is included, they are given the title of *Mu'awwidhat*, which means 'surahs of refuge or shelter.' Whenever the noble Messenger felt discomfort and also every night before going to bed, he recited these three surahs above, blew in his hands and then wiped his body beginning from his head and face to as far as his hands could reach. He repeated the whole procedure three times.[27]

In *Surah Falaq* refuge in God is sought from all evil. Then, the extreme cases of evil are emphasized and it is recommended to seek refuge in God from the evil of the darkness of night, from the evil of witches who cast spells by blowing and spitting on knots, and from the envy of those who are possessed by envy. In *Surah Nas*, following the recitation of the Divine names 'Lord,' 'Sovereign,' and 'Deity of humankind,' we seek refuge from those among human beings and jinn who sinisterly whisper evil into hearts.

Satan is the first of those from whom we must take refuge in God, since he plans to whisper deception and evil thoughts into hearts at the most unexpected times. He brings various thoughts to mind even during the recitation of the Qur'an. He tries to occupy the mind with issues not related to the Qur'an. He attempts to infiltrate the mind with suspicion regarding the holy verses. Using various other methods, he tries to pull people away from the atmosphere of the Qur'an. Almighty God instructs us to take refuge in Him, prior to reciting the Qur'an: "*When you recite the Qur'an, seek refuge in God from Satan rejected*" (Nahl 16:98), reminding us that even during recitation, we are vulnerable to the suggestions and whisperings of the evil one. Seeking refuge in God is a command; so, one must seek refuge from Satan in order to benefit from the holy Qur'an. Essentially, this is an act of the heart. This is why most scholars have regarded the recitation of the word *a'udhu* as *mustahab* (recommended) instead of classifying it as *wajib* (necessary).

Taking refuge in God from the evil one also means putting one's trust in God. Asking for God's protection from the archenemy of humankind also proves one's confidence in God. One who seeks shelter in God is aware of the fact that His power is infinite. God will protect us from Satan if it is requested. There is a verse which clarifies this: *"Surely he (Satan) has no power over those who believe and put their trust in their Lord"* (Nahl 16:99).

It is interesting that God addresses the Prophet when He explains the issue of taking refuge. A person whose Satan has surrendered would not pursue other thoughts when reciting the Qur'an. However, to emphasize the importance of the matter, God used this particular method of cautioning even the noble Messenger about it. Just like the Qur'an, the noble Prophet also takes the matter very seriously and instructs us to take refuge in God. As a matter of fact, he acted as a role model to his followers by seeking refuge in God and asking for His protection from the evil one.

Prayers and *istiadha* had a vital place in his life. There is a prayer and an appeal to the Almighty in every chapter of his life. Here we will give a few examples of his prayers and *istiadha*:

a. The noble Prophet said, "Satan may approach one of you and ask, 'Who created this and who created that?' and then he may ask, 'Who created God?' Whoever falls into such a situation should quickly seek refuge in God and snap out of it."[28]

b. The noble Prophet stated, "Both the angel and Satan possess the ability of inculcation. Satan pledges evil and renounces the truth, whilst the angel promises virtue and confirms the truth. Whoever feels this in their conscience (the angel's suggestion), should praise God. Whoever senses the other (Satan's whisper) should quickly seek refuge in God from Satan, the rejected one." The noble Prophet concluded by reciting the following verse: *"Satan frightens you with poverty and bids you into indecencies"* (Baqara 2:268).[29]

c. Abu Bakr said, "O Messenger of God, tell me something (a prayer) I can recite day and night." The Prophet replied, "O the Knower of the unseen and the seen, the Creator of the heavens and the earth, the Possessor and Maintainer of all! I testify that there is no god other than You. I seek refuge in You from my carnal soul, Satan, and falling into hypocrisy." Then, God's Messenger continued, "Recite this in the day, and at night when you lie on your bed."[30]

d. The noble Prophet also took refuge in God from Satan's deception at the time of death. As well as seeking refuge from falling, being crushed under rubble, drowning and burning, he also pleaded with God, "I seek refuge in You from Satan's strike at the time of death."[31]

e. Every time the noble Messenger entered the Masjid, he would recite, "I seek refuge in Almighty God, in the exalted One and in His eternal Throne from Satan, the rejected."[32] It is very meaningful that the Messenger pleaded for protection even as he entered the Masjid.

f. The noble Prophet states, "Before you approach your wives, you should say, 'O God! Keep Satan away from me and the child You shall grant.' When you recite this, if you are blessed with a child, both you and your child will be protected from Satan."[33]

EATING LESS

One practical defense strategy against Satan's attacks is controlling our eating habits. Controlling eating habits is a basic principle of a healthy, comfortable, efficient and energetic life. A controlled diet is the most important step toward a healthy life. Nevertheless, no matter what precautions we take, we must all at some point in our lives suffer from illness. However, we all know that overeating is an invitation to various ailments. Being overweight also affects our psychological health. Even our finances can receive a hefty blow due to obesity-related illnesses. There are quite a number of people who spend significant amounts of money on attempts to lose weight, even if they have no health complaints. As a matter of fact, to some people, losing weight seems the most important issue in life.

Just as it affects our worldly life in a negative way, overeating also impinges on our religious life. It causes problems such as sleeping too much, weariness, indiscreet talk, exaggerated laughter, memory loss, and unwillingness to worship. In contrast, those who manage to control their diet become more dynamic, enthusiastic, sharp, and alert. Their hearts shine brilliantly and they are sensitive and keen in their prayers. A controlled diet narrows Satan's field of play, enabling us to be more cautious against him.

Lust is one of Satan's greatest weapons, and the best way to control it is by lowering the body's calorie intake. The noble Prophet advised marriage to those who could afford it, and to others he recommended fasting so that they could control their sexual desires.[34]

Imam Ghazali lists the benefits of a controlled diet:

- It strengthens the memory and causes the heart to glow and open. A full stomach, on the other hand, makes one thick-headed and blinds the eye of the heart. It reduces the level of one's ability to comprehend.

- It develops tenderness in the heart, causing it to become more sensitive and soft. It helps us understand our own weakness, which causes us to turn to God. It also helps us to perceive our own deficiency and to feel the power and grace of our Lord in our conscience.

- It causes people to become more aware of what is going on around them. Incidents begin to make a place in their conscience, causing them to derive a lesson from everything. Their compassion toward the needy increases.

- It decreases the amount of sleep, which would otherwise gradually eat a person's life away.

- It supports the continuation of prayers.

- It helps a person to lead a healthy, ailment-free life by supporting the well being of the body.
- It helps people to budget and economize, so that those in poverty may also be supported.
- It breaks the emotions of lust and evil desires. Lust is one of the major desires which drag people into rebellion against God. Every organ in the human body possesses some form of lust. However, the most powerful of them is the lust felt toward the opposite sex. A controlled diet and fasting is the best form of defense which breaks these inclinations or minimizes their effect.[35]

People cannot control their desires when they fill their stomachs to the top. The desires for the opposite sex and a full stomach are proportional to each other. The more food one consumes, the hungrier one's lust becomes and vice versa. Many people in the world face the troublesome consequences of their negligence regarding this issue. Obesity has become a major problem, causing many people to spend their lives on strict diets. In some situations, this lack of control has caused some to deviate from the straight path, leaving them in shame and difficulties, even though, with discipline and self-control, it is possible for one to protect oneself from various problems and at the same time enhance one's spiritual life. Yet, it is quite difficult to lead a life contrary to Satan and opposing the desires of the carnal soul. It seems that those who fail to overcome this difficulty will eventually destroy both their current worlds and the one after.

We can also look at this issue from another perspective. As Bediüzzaman Said Nursi said, "Good deeds have detrimental obstacles. Satans frequently pester those who serve this cause."[36] As a matter of fact, Satan cannot bear to see even one individual establish strong bonds with his or her Lord. Consequently, it is not surprising that satans lose their minds in the presence of people uniting in harmony to serve Islam, the religion of God.

Conclusion

Humankind is in trouble with Satan. He touches every newborn. He tries to deceive every young person by decorating sins and presenting them before their eyes. Not only does he pester humans throughout the day, he also looks for ways to manipulate their dreams. He approaches them during prayer, hoping to make them lose concentration. He sticks his nose into the most private parts of life. He approaches men and women even at the time of death, trying to destroy their eternity. He is the greatest enemy of humankind, and he is devious, extremely sinister, and a compulsive liar.

We can summarize his character like this:

- He is arrogant, egoistic and has a rebellious soul.
- Upon hearing the Divine command, he failed to overcome his emotions, and so all his evil feelings surfaced. He rebelled and was cursed by the wrath of God.
- He blamed Adam for everything, assuming that Adam was responsible for all that happened, and thus he became man's archenemy and swore vengeance against Adam and his descendants.
- Satan is at fault for becoming an enemy to Adam as much as he was at fault for disobeying God's command.
- When he disobeyed the command, he became a rebel against God. Moreover, he made things worse when he attempted to defend himself by justifying his actions. His rebellion caused him to be rejected and distanced from Divine Mercy, and being away from Mercy brought upon him the gradual decomposition of all that he possessed of good. Consequently, he found himself in a vicious circle where all doors leading to good had been permanently locked up.
- Satan was not deprived of mercy when he was created, but he brought God's wrath upon himself by using his abilities for the wrong reasons.

- He chooses companions among man and jinn who have killed off their souls, ruined their consciences and destroyed their nature.
- Satan will display his biggest act of disloyalty by leaving those who have followed him all alone with their fate on the Day of Judgment.
- On the Day of Judgment, when the infinite mercy of the Almighty prevails, even Satan will develop hope and vainly look for ways to repent. Contrarily, Satan survives with the hope that God may forgive him at the end. This is called, "Satan's hope of paradise."[37]

The prescription for protection from Satan's evil is provided by the holy Qur'an and Sunna. As long as these sacred sources are adopted—by the will of God—his influence will be broken and humankind will find eternal joy by living a life on the horizons of pleasing God.

NOTES

INTRODUCTION

1   Fethullah Gülen, *Fasıldan Fasıla*, Vol. IV, 40.

1

THE CREATION AND ESSENCE OF SATAN

1   Abu Dawud, *Sunan*, Hadith no. 4766.

2   Bukhari, *Sahih Bukhari*, 8.136.

3   See the entry for *"sh-t-n"* in Ibn Manzur, *Lisan al-Arab*; Raghib Isfahani, *Al-Mufradat*; Asım Efendi, *Qamus*.

4   Yazır, *Hak Dini Kur'an Dili*, II, 238.

5   See the entry for *"Shaitan,"* in Asım Efendi, *Qamus*.

6   See the entry for *"b-l-s,"* in Ibn Manzur, ibid.; Zabidi, *Taj al-Arus*.

7   Sa'd 38:76; A'raf 7:12.

8   Konuk, *Fususu'l-Hikem, Tercüme ve Şerhi*, (Annotated Interpretation of Ibn al-Arabi's *Fusus al-Hikam*), I, 30.

9   See also Hijr 15:29–40 and Sa'd 38:75–76.

10 See Yazır, ibid., III. 2130–2134.

11 Gülen, *Asrın Getirdiği Tereddütler*, II, 47.

12 Darimi, *Sunan, Muqaddama*, 22.

13 Darimi, ibid.

14 Yazır, ibid., III, 2029.

15 Nasai, *Sunan, Istiadha*, 48; Ahmad ibn Hanbal, *Musnad*, V. 178–265.

16 Ateş, *Yüce Kur'an'ın Çağdaş Tefsiri*, III, 223.

17 Yazır, ibid., II, 237.

18 Yazır, ibid., V, 3059.

19 Muslim, *Birr*, 111; Ahmad ibn Hanbal, *Musnad*, III, 240–254.

20 See Qiyama 75:36; Sad 38:27; Shu'ara 26:128.

21 See Furqan 25:39.

22 See Gülen, *Prizma*, I, 155.

23 Abu Bakr (d. 634) was one of the first Muslims, the Prophet's Companion during his migration to Medina, and the first caliph after the Prophet's death. He has always been remembered for his attachment to the Prophet and support for him, truthfulness, and simple life. Abu Jahl (lit. 'Father

of Ignorance'), on the other hand, was one of the Prophet's main opponents who fought him at every turn and was killed in the Battle of Badr.

24 Said Nursi, *The Letters, Risale-i Nur Collection*, 71–72.

25 See the entry of 's-c-d' in Zabidi's *Taj al-Arus*; Elmalılı Hamdi Yazır, ibid., I, 318.

26 See Baqara 2:34; Hijr 15:30; Isra 17:61.

27 See Yusuf 12:100.

28 Zamakhshari, *Kashshaf*, I, 130.

29 Ibn Maja, *Zuhd*, 30.

30 Gülen, *Varlığın Metafizik Boyutu*.

31 Tabari, *Jami al-Bayan*, I, 232–233; Baydawi, *Anwar al-Tanzil*, I, 54; Qurtubi, *Al Jami'li Ahkam al-Qur'an*, I, 2208–2209.

2

SATAN AS MENTIONED IN THE QUR'AN AND HADITH

1 See Yusuf 12:5; Isra 17:53; Zukhruf 43:62.

2 See Baqara 2:268.

3 Yazır, ibid., VI, 4100.

4 Zamakhshari, ibid., I, 172; Alusi, *Ruh al-Maani*, I. 338; Ibn al-Jawzi, *Zad al-Masir*, I, 120; Elmalılı Hamdi Yazır, ibid., I, 440–441.

5 Yazır, ibid., I, 439–440.

6 See Nas 114:6.

7 Zamakhshari, ibid., IV, 565; Baydawi, *Anwar al-Tanzil wa Asrar al-Ta'wil*, II, 290.

8 Yazır, ibid., VIII, 5404.

9 Osman Efendi, *Dürretül-Vâizin*, 71.

10 Bukhari, *Hudud*, 5; Ahmad ibn Hanbal, *Musnad*, II, 300.

11 See the entry for *najwa*, Asım Efendi, *Qamus*.

12 See the entry for 'n-j-w,' Ibn Manzur, ibid..

13 Bukhari, *Isti'zan*, 47; Muslim, *Salaam*, 37, 38; Tirmidhi, *Adab*, 59; Ibn Maja, *Tahara*, 24

14 Yazır, ibid., XII, 4790.

15 See Isra 17:62.

16 Yazır, ibid., III, 1805.

17 Nuraddin Itr, *Manhaj an-Nakd*, 26.

18 Bukhari, *Adab*, 70; Ibn Maja, *Mukaddama*, 7.

19 Bukhari, *Bad al-Khalq*, 11; *Adab*, 121; *Itikaf*, 11–12; Muslim, *Salaam*, 23–24.

20   Nawawi, *Sharh al-Sahih Muslim*, XIV, 157; Davudoğlu, *Sahihi Müslim Tercüme ve Şerhi* (Annotated Interpretation of Sahih Muslim), IX, 244–245; Aliyy al-Qari, *Mirqat*, V.

21   Bukhari, *Bad al-Khalq*, 11; Muslim, *Tahara*, 27.

22   Nawawi, ibid., III, 127–128.

23   Nawawi, ibid.

24   Ibn Hanbal, *Musnad*, V, 60; Muttaqi, *Kanz al-Ummal*, 28567.

25   Muslim, *Zuhd*, 56.

26   Ibn Hanbal, *Musnad*, III, 31, 93, 96; Abu Dawud, *Adab*, 97.

27   Webster Dictionary.

28   Ateş, *Şeytan*, 221

29   Bukhari, *Adab*, 2, 10; Muslim, *Birr*, 106–108; Malik, *Muwatta*, Husn al-Khuluq, 12.

30   Bukhari, *Ilm*, 28; *Luqata*, 9; *Adab* 75; Muslim, *Luqata*, 2,7; Tirmidhi, *Qadar*, 1; Ibn Maja, *Masajid*, 10; Nasai, *Masajid*, 35.

31   Al-Asqalani, *Fath al-Bari*, X, 535.

32   Bukhari, *Bad al-Khalq*, 11; Tirmidhi, *Nikah*, 8.

33   Gülen, *Varlığın Metafizik Boyutu*.

34   Bukhari, *Bad al-Khalq*, 11; Muslim, Fadail, 146–148.

35   Nawawi, ibid., XV, 129.

36   Muslim, *Masajid*, 196; Abu Dawud, *Salat*, 5; Tirmidhi, *Salat*, 120.

37   Muslim, *Salat al-Musafirin wa Kasruha*; Nasai, *Mawakit*, 35.

38   Bukhari, *Bad al-Khalq*, 11; Muslim, *Salat al-Musafirin wa Kasruha*, 290.

39   Nawawi, ibid., VI, 361.

40   Bukhari, *Bad al-Khalq*, 11; Muslim, *Fitan*, 45–50; Tirmidhi, *Fitan*, 79.

41   Bukhari, *Fitan*, 16; Tirmidhi, *Manakib*, 75.

42   Bukhari, *Khums*, 4.

43   Ayni, *Umdat al-Qari Sharh al-Sahih Bukhari*, XX, 84.

44   Muslim, *Ashriba*, 104–106; Abu Dawud, *At'ima*, 20.

45   Abu Dawud, *At'ima*, 15; Ahmad ibn Hanbal, *Musnad*, IV, 336.

46   Muslim, *Ashriba*, 102; Abu Dawud, *At'ima*, 16.

47   Muslim, *Ashriba*, 135–137; Abu Dawud, *A'tima*, 50; Tirmidhi, *A'tima*, 11.

48   Ibn Manzur, ibid., see the entry for 'r-a-y.'

49   Bukhari, *Bad al-Khalq*, 11; Muslim, *Ruya*, 1,2; Abu Dawud, *Adab*, 96.

50   Muslim, *Ruya*, 3.

51   Muslim, *Ruya*, 14–16; Ibn Maja, *Kitab al-Tabir al-Ruya*, 35.

52   Yazır, ibid., IV, 2866.

53   Bukhari, *Tabir*, 2,4,10, 26; Muslim, *Ruya*, 6–9; Abu Dawud, *Adab*, 44; Tirmidhi, *Ruya*, 6–7–10; Ibn Maja, *Ruya*, 1, 3, 6, 9.

54   Bukhari, *Tabir*, 26; Muslim, *Ruya*, 6; Abu Dawud, *Adab*, 96.

55   Bukhari, *Tabir*, 10; Muslim, *Ruya*, 10; Abu Dawud, *Adab, 96.*

56   Ibn Hajar, ibid., XII, 403; Nawawi, ibid., XV, 31.

57   Abu Dawud, *Jihad*, 79; Tirmidhi, *Jihad*, 4; Ahmad ibn Hanbal, *Musnad*, II, 186.214.

58   Azimabadi, *Awn al-Mabud*, VII, 266; Mubaraq al-Furi, *Tuhfat al-Ahwazi*, V, 319.

59   Muslim, *Ashriba*, 98; Abu Dawud, *Jihad*, 76; Ahmad ibn Hanbal, *Musnad*, III, 362, 395.

60   Bukhari, *Bad al-Khalq*, 11, 15; Muslim, *Ashriba*, 97.

61   Muslim, *Ashriba*, 103; Abu Dawud, *A'tima*, 15; Ibn Maja, *Dua*, 19.

62   Bukhari, *Bad al-Khalq*, 11; *Adab*, 68; Muslim, *Fadail al-Sahaba*, 22.

63   Tirmidhi, *Manakib*, 17; Ahmad ibn Hanbal, *Musnad*, V, 353.

64   Nawawi, *Sharh al-Sahih Muslim*, XV, 174.

65   Ahmad ibn Hanbal, *Musnad*, V, 104.

66   Bukhari, *Wudu*, 73; Muslim, *Tahara*, 46.

67   Bukhari, *Jum'a*, 8; Muslim, *Tahara*, 42.

68   Nasai, *Ishrat al-Nisa*, 10; Ahmad ibn Hanbal, *Musnad*, III, 128.

69   Malik, *Muwatta*, *Sha'r*, 2.

70   Muslim, *Libas*, 41; Abu Dawud, *Libas*, 45; Nasai, *Nikah*, 82.

71   Tirmidhi, *Birr*, 66.

72   Bukhari, *Bad al-Khalq*, 11; Tirmidhi, *Daawat*, 57; Abu Dawud, *Adab*, 115.

73   Muslim, *Libas*, 104; Ahmad ibn Hanbal, *Musnad*, II, 366.

74   Muslim, *Janaiz*, 10; Ahmad ibn Hanbal, *Musnad*, VI, 289.

75   Tirmidhi, *Rada'*, 16; Ahmad ibn Hanbal, *Musnad*, I, 18, 26.

76   Abu Dawud, *Tahara*, 72; Tirmidhi, *Tahara*, 44.

77   Muslim, *Salat*, 265; Abu Dawud, *Salat*, 110; Tirmidhi, *Salat*, 253.

3

SATAN'S ATTRIBUTES, METHODS AND INFESTATION OF THE HEART

1   Yazır, ibid., III, 2142.

2   Yazır, ibid., III, 2143.

3   Baydawi, *Anwar al-Tanzil*, I, 99.

4   Raghib, *Mufradat*, see the entry for '*h-w-n*.'

5   Devellioğlu, *Osmanlıca–Türkçe Ansiklopedik Lugat*, the entry for '*hizlan*.'

6   An'am 6:153.

7   Ibn Hanbal, *Musnad*, I, 435.

8   Ibn Manzur, ibid., see the entry for '*w-s-w*'; Raghib, ibid., the entry for '*w-s-w*.'

9   Ibn Manzur, ibid., see the entry for '*h-n-s*.'

10 Raghib, ibid., see the entry for '*h-n-s*.'

11 Aliyy al-Qari, ibid., V, 66.

12 See A'raf 7:20; Ta Ha 20:120.

13 Baydawi, *Anwar al-Tanzil*, I, 54; Elmalılı Hamdi Yazır, ibid., III, 2141.

14 Ibn Hanbal, *Musnad*, III, 483.

15 Muslim, *Ashriba*, 174; Ahmad ibn Hanbal, *Musnad*, VI, 2–3.

16 Baqara 2:255.

17 Bukhari, *Wakalat*, 10; *Fadail al-Qur'an*, 10.

18 Muslim, *Sifat al-Munafikin wa Ahkamuhum*, 16.

19 Qutb, *Fi Zilal al-Qur'an*, III, 1531

20 Said Nursi, *Al-Mathnawi Al-Nuri*, The Fifth Treatise, Risale-i Nur Collection.

21 Muslim, *Iman*, 211; *Musnad*, 2/256.

22 Gülen, *Varlığın Metafizik Boyutu*.

23 Ibn Manzur, ibid., entry for '*l-a-n*.'

24 Asım Efendi, Qamus, entry for '*lanat*.'

25 Zumar 39:7.

26 Tawba 9:71.

27 Ibn Manzur, ibid., the entry for '*a-s-y*.'

28 Maryam 19:44.

29 Yazır, ibid., III, 2148.

30 Raghib, ibid., the entry for '*z-y-n*.'

31 See Imran 3:14; Tawba 9:37; Baqara 2:212.

32 Yazır, ibid., II, 1051.

33 Ibn al-Jawzi, *Talbis al-Iblis*, 36.

34 Ibn Maja, *Talaq*, 16.

35 Yazır, ibid., II, 1003.

36 Abu Dawud, *Nikah*, 49; Ahmad ibn Hanbal, *Musnad*, II, 541.

37 Yazır, ibid., II, 957.

38 Qurtubi, ibid., IV, 135.

39 Yazır, ibid., VI, 3100.

40 Razi, ibid., VII, 90.

41 Baydawi, ibid., I, 142.

42 Ibn Manzur, ibid., entry for '*sh-h-y*.'

43 Muslim, *Birr*, 14, 15; Tirmidhi, *Zuhd*, 56.

44 Bukhari, *Nikah*, 17; Tirmidhi, *Adab*, 31; *Zuhd*, 56.

45 Muslim, *Nikah*, 9; Tirmidhi, *Rada'*, 9.

46 Nawawi, ibid., IX, 188.

47 Bukhari, *Nikah*, 8; Muslim, *Nikah*, 6–8.

48   Ibn Manzur, ibid., entry for '*sh-h-r*.'

49   Ghazali, *Ihya*, III, 404.

50   Ghazali, *Ihya*, III, 444.

51   See Maun 107:4–7.

52   Yazır, ibid.,V, 3415.

53   Muslim, *Dhikr*, 41; Abu Dawud, *Witr*, 26.

54   Muslim, *Dhikr*, 41; Abu Dawud, *Witr*, 26.

55   Yazır, ibid., IX, 6404.

56   Bukhari, *Bad al-Khalq*, 8; *Tawhid*, 35; Muslim, *Iman*, 213; *Janna*, 2–5.

57   Ghazali, *Ihya*, III, 43.

58   Bukhari, *Iman*, 39; Muslim, *Musakat*, 107.

59   Tirmidhi, *Qadar*, 7; Ahmad ibn Hanbal, *Musnad*, IV, 302.

60   Gülen, *Kalbin Zümrüt Tepeleri*, I, 48.

61   Yazır, ibid., I, 210.

62   Qutb, *Fi Zilal al-Qur'an*.

63   Ibn Kathir, *Tafsir li'l Qur'an al-Azim*, I, 467.

64   Raghıb, *Mufradat*, entry for '*m-r-d*.'

65   Tirmidhi, *Kitab al-Tafsir al-Qur'an*, 2.

4

SATAN'S EXPLOITATION OF WORSHIP

1   Ibn Hanbal, *Musnad*, II, 380.

2   Bukhari, *Kitab at-Tafsir*, 43.

3   Bukhari, *Iman*, 37; Muslim, *Iman*, 57.

4   Muslim, *Iman*, 133.

5   Ibn Hanbal, *Musnad*, V, 136.

6   Muttaqi, *Kanz al-Ummal*, IX, 26260.

7   Ibn Hanbal, *Musnad*, II, 330.

8   Bukhari, *Hayd*, 98–99; *Wudu*, 4–34; *Buyu*, 5; Abu Dawud, *Tahara*, 67; Nasai, *Tahara*, 114.

9   Bukhari, *Bad al-Khalq*, 11.

10   Ibn Hanbal, *Musnad*, III, 154.

11   Abu Dawud, *Salat*, 2.

12   Bukhari, *Bad al-Khalq*, 11.

13   Ayni, ibid., V, 51.

14   Muslim, *Salat*, 38–40; Abu Dawud, *Salat*, 132.

15   Bukhari, *Salat*, 75; Muslim, *Masajid*, 39.

16   Ibn Hanbal, *Musnad*, III, 471.

17 Ibn Hanbal, *Musnad*, II, 161–205; Abu Dawud, *Adab*, 109; Bukhari, *Adhan*, 155; Muslim, *Dhikr*, 81.

18 Bukhari, *Bad al-Khalq*, 11.

19 Kari, *Mirqat*, III, 295.

20 Miras, *Tecrid-i Sarih Tercüme ve Şerhi*, IV, 159.

21 Al-Farisi, *Al-Ihsan*, VI, 2588.

22 Bukhari, *Bad al-Khalq*, 11; *Tahajjud*, 13; Muslim, *Musafirin*, 205.

23 Tahawi, *Sharh al-Mushkil al-Asar*, X, 144.

24 Nawawi, ibid., VI, 310; Kamil Miras, *Tecrid-i Sarih Tercüme ve Şerhi*, VIII, 111.

25 Muslim, *Masajid*, 310; Nasai, *Mawakit*, 55.

26 Bukhari, *Salat*, 16; *Libas*, 12; Muslim, *Libas*, 23; Ibn Maja, *Qibla*, 19.

27 Zihni Efendi, *Nimet-i İslam*.

28 Zuhayli, *Al-Fıqh al-Islami*, I, 752.

29 Bukhari, *Salat*, 39; Muslim, *Salat*, 258–260.

30 Abu Dawud, *Salat*, 107; Nasai, *Qibla*, 5.

31 Nawawi, ibid., IV, 471.

32 Ateş, ibid., 198.

33 Abu Dawud, *Salat*, 190; Ibn Maja, *Iqama*, 132.

34 Bukhari, *Sawm*, 2; *Tawhid*, 35; *Libas*, 78; Muslim, *Siyam*, 41; Ibn Maja, *Adab*, 58.

35 Bukhari, *Sawm*, 2; *Tawhid*, 35; Muslim, *Siyam*, 162–163.

36 Bukhari, *Sawm*, 5; Muslim, *Siyam*, 1; Tirmidhi, *Sawm*, 1.

37 Nawawi, ibid., VII, 194.

38 Ayni, ibid., IX, 22.

39 Ibn Hajar, ibid., IV, 137; Davudoglu, ibid., VI, 13.

40 Zuhayli, ibid., III, 8.

41 Zihni Efendi, *Nimeti İslam*, 627.

42 Tabari, *Tarih al-Umam*, I, 260.

43 Zuhayli, ibid., II, 730.

44 Zuhayli, ibid., II, 732.

45 Yazır, ibid., II, 913.

46 Bukhari, *Zakat*, 11; Muslim, *Zakat*, 92–93.

5

MEANS OF PROTECTION

1 Gülen, *Varlığın Metafizik Boyutu*.

2 Yazır, ibid., I, 196–197.

3   Yazır, ibid., I, 95.

4   Raghib, *Mufradat*, the entry for '*a-b-d*.'

5   Dhariat 51:56.

6   Bukhari, *Rikak*, 38; Ahmad ibn Hanbal, *Musnad*, II, 256.

7   Bukhari, *Tawhid*, 15, 50; Muslim, *Dhikr*, 20–22; Tirmidhi, *Daawat*, 131.

8   Zarkani, *Manahil al-Irfan fi Ulum al-Qur'an.*, I, 19.

9   Yazır, ibid., V, 3195; Tabari, ibid., XV. 152

10 Darimi, *Fadail al-Qur'an*, I.

11 Darimi, ibid.

12 Muslim, *Musafirin*, 212; Tirmidhi, *Kitab al-Fadail al-Qur'an*, 2.

13 Tirmidhi, *Kitab al-Fadail al-Qur'an*, 4; Ahmad ibn Hanbal, *Musnad*, IV, 274.

14 Bukhari, *Ijara*, 16; Tirmidhi, *Tib*, 20.

15 Raghib, *Mufradat*, the entry for '*w-k-y*;' Ibn Manzur, ibid., the entry for '*w-k-y*.'

16 Gülen, *Kalbin Zümrüt Tepeleri*, 75.

17 Jurjani, *Tarifat*, *Iman*.

18 Ibn Maja, *Zuhd*, 24; Tirmidhi, *Kıyama*, 19.

19 Nursi, *Lem'alar*, *Risale-i Nur Collection*, 72.

20 Gülen, *Asrın Getirdiği Tereddütler*, IV, 180–181.

21 Gülen, ibid., IV, 182–183.

22 See A'raf 7:200; Fussilat 41:36.

23 Munjid, *Dar al-Mashrik*, the entry for '*a-w-z*.'

24 Nursi, *Lem'alar*, *Risale-i Nur Collection*, 70–71.

25 See Yusuf 12:23.

26 See Yusuf 12:79.

27 Bukhari, *Fadail al-Qur'an*, 15; Tirmidhi, *Dua*, 21; Ibn Maja, *Dua*, 12.

28 Bukhari, *Bad al-Khalq*, 11; Muslim, *Iman*, 213–214.

29 Tirmidhi, *Tafsir al-Qur'an*, 36.

30 Tirmidhi, *Daawat*, 14.

31 Abu Dawud, *Witr*, 32.

32 Abu Dawud, *Salat*, 18.

33 Bukhari, *Bad al-Khalq*, 11; Muslim, *Nikah*, 116.

34 Bukhari, *Sawm*, 10; Muslim, *Nikah*, 1–3.

35 Ghazali, *Ihya*, III, 128–134.

36 Nursi, *Risale-i Nur Collection*, *Lemalar*, 222.

37 Mansur, *Mawaid al-Shaitan*, 11.

BIBLIOGRAPHY

Abdul Baqi, Muhammad Fuad, *Al-Mu'jam al-Mufahras li al-Fazi'l-Qur'an al-Karim*, Çağrı Yayınları: Istanbul, 1990.

Abdul Hakim, Mansur, *Mawaid al-Shaitan*, Dar al-Ranida: Cairo, 1993.

Abu Dawud, Sulayman ibn Al-Askhas al-Sijistani, *Sunan Abu Dawud*, I–IV, Al-Maktabat al-Islamiyya: Istanbul, 1315ah.

Ajluni, Ismail ibn Muhammad al-Jarahi, *Kashf al-Khafa wa Muzhil al-Ilbas Amma'sh-Tahara min al-Ahadisi ala Alsinat al-Nas*, Dar al-Kutub al-Ilmiyya: Beirut, 1988.

Aliyy al-Qari, *Mirqat al-Mafatih Sharhu Mishkat al-Masabih*, I–X, Dar al-Fikr: Beirut, 1992.

Alusi, Abu al-Fadl Shihabuddin al-Sayyid Mahmud al-Baghdadi, *Ruh al-Maani Fi Tafsir al-Qur'an al-Azim*, I–XXX, Dar al-Ihya al-Turas al-Arabi: Beirut, 1985.

AnaBritannica, I–XXXII, Ana Yayıncılık A.Ş: Istanbul, 1986.

Asım Efendi, *Qamus*, I–IV, Cemal Efendi Matbaası: Istanbul, 1305ah.

Asqalani, Ahmad ibn Ali ibn Hajar, *Fath al-Bari fi Sharh al-Sahih Bukhari*, I–XII, Dar al-Bayan: Egypt, 1988.

Ateş, Ali Osman, *Kur'an ve Hadislere Göre Şeytan*, (*Satan Described in the Qur'an and Hadith*), Beyan Yayınları: Istanbul, 1989.

Ateş, Süleyman, *Yüce Kur'an'ın Çağdaş Tefsiri*, (*Exegesis of the Glorious Qur'an*), I–XII, Yeni Ufuklar Neşriyat: Istanbul, 1989.

Ayni, Badraddin Abu Muhammad ibn Ahmad, *Umdat al-Qari Sharh al-Sahih Bukhari*, I–XX, Matbaat al-Mustafa al-Babi al-Halabi: Egypt, 1972.

Azimabadi, Abu al-Tiyb Muhammad al-Shams al-Haqq, *Awn al-Ma'bud Sharhu Sunan Abu Dawud*, I–XIV, Matkabat al-Salafiya: Medina, 1968.

Baydawi, Al-Qadi Abdu'llah ibn Umar, *Anwar al-Tanzil wa Asrar al-Ta'wil*, I–II, Dar al-Kutub al-Ilmiyya: Beirut, 1988.

Bukhari, Muhammad ibn Ismail, *Sahih al-Bukhari*, I–VIII, Al-Maktabat al-Islamiyya: Istanbul, 1315ah.

Büyük Türkçe Sözlük, Türk Dil Kurumu: Ankara, 1988.

Darimi, Abu Muhammad ibn Abdul Rahman ibn Fadl, *Sunan al-Darimi*, I–II, Matbaat al-I'tidal: Damascus, 1349ah.

Davudoğlu, Ahmed, *Sahih-i Müslim Tercüme ve Şerhi*, (*Annotated Interpretation of Sahih Muslim*), I–XII, Sönmez Neşriyat: Istanbul, 1977.

Devellioğlu, Ferid, *Osmanlıca–Türkçe Ansiklopedik Lügat*, Aydın Yayınları: Ankara, 1993.

Doğan, Mehmet D., *Büyük Türkçe Sözlük*, Ülke Yayıncılık, Haber Ticaret Ltd. Şti.: Istanbul, 1994.

Farisi, Ibn Balban al-Farisi, *Al-Ihsan fi Taqribi Sahih ibn Hibban*, I–XVIII, (Edition Critique by Shuayb al-Arnawut), Muassasat al-Risala: Beirut, 1988.

Fığlalı, Ethem Ruhi, *Çağımızda İtikadi İslam Mezhepleri*, Selçuk Yay: Ankara, 1990.

Ghazali, Abu Hamid Muhammad ibn Muhammad, *Ihya al-Ulum al-Din*, I–V, Dar al-Kutayba: Damascus, 1992.

Gölcük, Şerâfeddin & Süleyman Toprak, *Kelâm*, Tekin Yay: Konya, 1991.

Gülen, Fethullah, *Kalbin Zümrüt Tepeleri*, (trns as *"Emerald Hills of the Heart, Key Concepts in the Practice of Sufism I-III"*) Nil Yayınları: İzmir, 1994.

————— *Ölçü veya Yoldaki Işıklar*, I–II, (trns as *"Pearls of Wisdom"*), T. Ö.V. Yayınları: İzmir, 1993.

————— *Prizma*, I–II, Nil Yayınları: İzmir, 1995.

————— *İ'la-yı Kelimetullah veya Cihad*, Nil Yayınları: İzmir, 1996.

————— *Varlığın Metafizik Boyutu*, Feza Gazetecilik: Istanbul, 1998.

————— *Asrın Getirdiği Tereddütler*, I–IV, (trns as *"Questions & Answers about Islam I-II"*), Nil Yayınları: İzmir, 2004.

————— *Fasıldan Fasıla*, I–IV, Nil Yayınları: İzmir, 2001.

Hökelekli, Hayati, *Din Psikolojisi*, Türkiye Diyanet Vakfı Yayınları: Ankara, 1996.

Hujwiri, *Ali ibn Uthman, Kashf al-Mahjub*, (trns as *Hakikat Bilgisi*, ed. Süleyman Uludağ), Dergah Yayınları: Istanbul, 1982.

Itr, Nuraddin, *Manhaj al-Nakd fi Ulum al-Hadith*, Dar al-Fikr: Beirut, 1992.

Ibn Jawzi, Abu al-Faraj, Jamaladdin Abdul Rahman ibn Ali, *Zad al-Masir fi Ilmi al- Tafsir*, I–IX, Al-Maktabat al-Islami, 1987.

————— *Talbis al-Iblis*, Dar Ibn Haldun: Alexandria, undated.

Ibn Jawziyya, Ibn Kayyim Abdu'llah ibn Muhammad, *Ighathat al-Lahfan*, Dar al-Hadith: Cairo, undated.

Ibn Hanbal, Ahmad ibn Muhammad, *Musnad al-Imam Ahmad ibn Hanbal*, I–VIII, Al-Maktabat al-Islamiyya, Beirut. 1993.

Ibn Kathir, Imamuddin Abu al-Fida, *Tafsir Li'l-Qur'an al-Azim*, I–VIII, Dar al-Kahraman, Istanbul, 1984.

Ibn Maja, Abu Abdillah, Al-Qazwini, *Sunan Ibn Maja*, Dar al-Ihya al-Kutub al-Arabi, undated.

Ibn Manzur, Jamaluddin Abu al-Fadl Muhammad ibn Mukarram, *Lisan al-Arab*, I–XV, Dar al-Fikr, Beirut, 1994.

Isfahani, Husayn ibn Muhammad al-Raghib, *Al-Mufradat fi Gharib al-Qur'an*, Dar al-Kahraman: Istanbul, 1986.

İslam Ansiklopedisi, Türkiye Diyanet Vakfı: Istanbul, 1988.

Jurjani, Sharif Ali ibn Muhammad, *Kitab al-Tarifat*, undated.

Konuk, Ahmed Avni, *Fususu'l-Hikem Tercüme ve Şerhi*, I–IV, (*Annotated Interpretation of Ibn Arabi's Fusus al-Hikam"*), İlahiyat Fakültesi Vakfı Yayınları: Istanbul, 1994.

Malik ibn Anas, *Al-Muwatta*, I–II, Dar al-Hadith: Cairo, undated.

Meydan Larousse Büyük Lügat ve Ansiklopedi, I–XV, Meydan Yayınları: Istanbul, 1990.

Maydani, Abdul Ghani al-Ghunaymi, *Sharh al-Akidat al-Tahawiya*, Dar al-Fikr: Damascus, undated.

Miras, Kamil, *Tecrid-i Sarih Tercüme ve Şerhi*, I–XII, (*Annotated Interpretation of Tajrid al-Sarih*), Diyanet İşleri Yay: Ankara, 1985.

Muhasibi, Harith, *Al-Riaya li Huquqi'llah*, (trns. as *Kalb Hayatı* by Abdulhakim Yüce), Çağlayan Yay: İzmir, 1997.

Mubarakfuri, Abu al-Ali Muhammad Abdur Rahman ibn Abdir Rahim, *Tuhfat al-Ahwadhi bi Sharhi Jami al-Tirmidhi*, I–X, Muassasat al-Qurtuba: Cairo, undated.

Munjid, *Munjid Fi al-Lughati wa'l A'lam*, Dar al-Mashrik: Beirut, 1986.

Muslim, Abu Husayn ibn Hajjaj al-Qushayri, *Sahih Muslim*, I–V, Al-Maktabat al-Islamiyya: Istanbul, 1955.

Muttaqi, Alauddin Ali, *Kanz al-Ummal*, I–XVII, Muassasat al-Risala: Beirut, undated.

Nasai, Abu Abdir Rahman Ahmad ibn Shuayb, *Sunan al-Nasai bi Sharh al-Suyuti*, I–VIII, Dar al-Ihya al-Turas al-Arabi: Beirut, undated.

Nawawi, Muhyiddin, *Sharh al-Sahih Muslim*, I–XVIII, Dar al-Kalam: Beirut, 1987.

Nursi, Bediüzzaman Said, *The Letters*, Risale-i Nur Collection, The Light: NJ, 2007.

——— *Al-Mathnawi Al-Nuri*, (*Seedbed of the Light*), Risale-i Nur Collection, The Light: NJ, 2007.

——— *Lemalar*, (The Flashes), Risale-i Nur Collection, Envar Neşriyat: Istanbul, 1990.

Osman Efendi, *Dürretül-Vâizin*, Sena Yay, 1976.

Qurtubi, Abu Abdi'llah Muhammad ibn Ahmad, *Al-Jami li Ahkam al-Qur'an*, I–XX, Dar al-Kutub al-Ilmiyya: Beirut, 1988.

Qushayri, Abu al-Qasim Abdul Karim ibn Hawazin, *Al-Risala al-Qushayriyya*, Cairo, 1940.

Qutb, Sayyid, *Fi Zilal al-Qur'an*, I–VI, Dar al-Shuruq: Egypt, 1988.

Razi, Fakhruddin, *Mafatih al-Ghayb*, I–XXXII, Dar al-Ihya al-Turas al-Arabi: Beirut.

Sharqawi, Hasan, *Mu'jam Alfaz al-Sufiyya*, Muassasat al-Mukhtar: Cairo, 1987.

Suhrawardi, Abdul Qahir ibn Abdi'llah, *Kitab al-Awarif al-Maarif*, (trns. as *Gerçek Tasavvuf*, ed. Dilaver Selvi), Ümran Yay.: Istanbul, 1995.

Tabari, Abu Jafar Muhammad ibn Jarir, *Jami al-Bayan an Tafsir Ayi'l-Qur'an*, I–XXX, Matbaat al-Mustafa al-Bab al-Halabi: Egypt, 1968.

———— *Tarih al-Umam wa'l-Muluk*, I–XIII, Dar al-Fikr: Beirut, 1987.

Tahawi, Abu Jafar, *Sharh al-Mushkil al-Athar*, I–X, Muassasat al-Risala: Beirut, 1994.

Tasawwuf al-Islami, Issue 10, year 19, Cairo, 1997.

Tirmidhi, Abu Isa Muhammad ibn Isa, *Jami al-Sahih*, I–V, Dar al-Ihya al-Turas al-Arabi: Beirut, undated.

Yazır, Muhammed Hamdi, *Hak Dini Kur'an Dili*, (*The Qur'an, the Language of the True Religion*), I–X, Eser Neşriyat: Istanbul, 1979.

Zabidi, Muhibbuddin Abu Fayd al-Sayyid Muhammad Murtaza al-Husayni, *Taj al-Arus min Jawahir al-Qamus*, I–XX, Dar al-Fikr: Beirut, 1994.

———— *Ithaf al-Saadat al-Muttaqin bi Sharh al-Ihya al-Ulum al-Din*, I–X, Dar al-Fikr: Beirut, undated.

Zamakhshari, Abu al-Qasim Jaru'llah Mahmud ibn Umar, *Al-Kashshaf 'an Haqaiq al-Ghawamid al-Tanzil wa Uyun al-Aqawil fi Wujuh al-Ta'wil*, I–IV, Dar al-Kutub al-Ilmiyya: Beirut, 1995.

Zarkani, Muhammad Abdul Azim, *Manahil al-Irfan fi Ulum al-Qur'an*, I–II, Dar al-Ihya al-Kutub al-Arabi: Cairo, 1918.

Zihni Efendi, Hacı Mehmet, *Nimet-i İslam*, Sönmez Neşriyat: Istanbul, undated.

Zuhayli, Wahba, *Al-Fıqh al-Islam wa Adillatuhu*, I–IX, Dar al-Fikr, Damascus, 1989.

INDEX

A

Abraham, forefather of prophets, 24

Adam, vii, viii, 5, 6, 7, 8, 10, 11, 12, 14, 15, 16, 17, 18, 24, 30, 31, 47, 51, 52, 54, 56, 57, 60, 64, 65, 83, 93, 130; father of humanity, 12; created of clay, 6, 8, 51; *Safiyu'llah* ('the Chosen of God'), 17

a'la-yi illiyin, 116

anger, 3, 7, 35, 36, 37, 73

archenemy, 12, 51, 126, 130

arrogance, 6, 9, 12, 14, 56, 84, 103, 122, 124

Azazil, 4

C

companions of Satan, 32; Satan's party, 32, 76

compulsive liar, 130

controlled diet, 127, 128, 129

D

deception, 21, 32, 34, 42, 47, 52, 65, 71, 72, 73, 77, 80, 82, 83, 92, 94, 95, 98, 103, 117, 118, 125, 127; deception through whispers, 34

devil, 27, 29, 41, 67, 76, 92

Divine Names

Divine Names (Beautiful Names of God), *Al-Mudhill* (The All-Abasing), 5; *Ar-Rahman* (The All-Merciful), 24, 29, 65, 76, 123, 125; *Al-Wahhab* (The All-Bestowing), 26

dreams, types of, 42; authentic (good) dream, 42; suggestion of one's own mind, 42; satanic dream, 42; *hulm*, 41, 42

E

egotism, 15

envy, 82

extravagance, 45

F

false promises and pledges, 21, 53, 54, 68, 70

fame, 80

food consumption, 40; eat not using your left hand, 40; leave no food on your plate, 41; recite *basmala*, 40, 43

forbiden tree, 16, 17, 18, 52, 54, 123

fortune-telling, 28

G

games of chance, 22, 29, 32